Thoughts from Dad

The Joy and Freedom of
Taking Responsibility

David Edel

Dear Debby
Thank you for being a good friend! Wishing you health, happiness + prosperity
David

Thoughts from Dad

Published by Hats Off Books™
610 East Delano Street, Suite 104, Tucson, Arizona
85705 U.S.A.
www.hatsoffbooks.com

International Standard Book Number: 1-58736-3607
Library of Congress Control Number: 2004109018

This book is dedicated to my sons, Joshua and Micah. I'm proud of who you both are.

Any profits from this book will be allocated to further your educational or business pursuits.

CONTENTS

PREFACE

This work is my heartfelt attempt to provide some fatherly guidance. I obviously didn't receive any from my dad since, as you know, he died at the age of thirty-two, just prior to my first birthday. Most parents want their children to surpass them in every area. I am no different. In this work, it is my desire that you will find some keys to help you have more happiness, success, money, accomplishment, fulfillment, freedom, and of course love than I have experienced.

This book is about taking personal responsibility for our lives and the resulting sense of control and happiness that is attained by doing so. Throughout the book, I am speaking to the writer as much as to the reader. I certainly do not claim mastery of every point, yet I am compelled to share what are meaningful concepts to me, hopefully to your benefit.

ACKNOWLEDGEMENTS

I'd like to thank William Bonner; William Glasser, MD; David Icke; Daphne Rose Kingma; Tony Robbins; Florence Schinn; Bernie Siegal; the other authors that have been quoted in this book; my mom; and many others who have greatly influenced my life. The credit for this book goes to these great men and women who have and are contributing so very much to improve people's lives.

A very special thanks to Kimberly Joy Lake for your help and encouragement. You've done so much for me. Thankyou.

Warm thanks to Kevin Small, John Wade, and Brad Hunsaker for your support and enduring friendship.

Thank you to Laura Arbree for title and cover idea.

Successful Living

"In the final analysis, the one quality that all successful people have ...is the ability to take on responsibility."

—Michael Korda 1919–1973

We find the greatest peace and happiness when we take full responsibility for our lives. The healthiest way to look upon life is that we create our lives. We create the quality of our lives by our actions, our thoughts, and our attitude. Our thoughts and attitude toward life are more powerful than most tend to believe. James Allen, the author of *As You Think*, says, "...We think in secret, and it comes to pass, our world is but our looking glass." If we are bitter, we will always find plenty to be bitter about. If we complain, we will always find plenty to complain about. We can help ourselves have positive thoughts by ignoring negative thoughts, spending time with positive people, reading inspiring books, watching programs or movies of an encouraging nature, meditating, and expressing gratitude.

How we see the world has everything to do with our personal satisfaction and our quality of life. The identical situation experienced by various people can be interpreted very differently. Rick Warren's best-selling book titled *The Purpose-Driven Life* says it like this: "The same diamond looks different from different angles." You may have heard the story of two siblings raised by an irresponsible alcoholic parent. One became an irresponsible alcoholic (because that's what his parent was) and the other became a successful community leader because he recognized the negativity of his parent's life and would never want to emulate it.

While we certainly cannot control all the events in our lives, how we view events and how we respond to events is extremely important to our happiness. If something negative happens, accept it. Blaming anyone will not help the situation. In fact, blaming anyone else for what is happening in your life hands control of your life to that person. Introspect and analyze to see if there is anything that you did that may have brought on the event so as not to make a similar mistake in the future. Socrates stated that the unexamined life is not worth living. Find something that you can learn from the event, and suddenly it will start taking on a positive nature.

Interestingly, as John F. Kennedy pointed out, "When written in Chinese, the word 'crisis' is composed of two characters—one represents danger, and the other represents opportunity." It all depends on how you look at it. Avoid the "woe is me," pity party like the plague (a theme that will be repeated throughout this book). A famous quote from Napoleon Hill, the author of *Think and Grow Rich* (the best selling book of all time second only to the Bible), says that, "Every adversity, every failure, and every heartache carries with it the seed of an equivalent or greater benefit."

Victor or victim? Our choice. We are caught in no one's web. We are bound by no circumstance. We are victims to no conditions. None of our behavior is caused by what happens outside of ourselves. There is no mental state in the world more pathetic than that of victim. The vic-

tim is saying, "I am innocent and helpless, totally dependent on what you do."

There is nothing out there!

Don't fool yourself into thinking that something outside of yourself is the cause of any of
your worries or troubles.

We are the authors of our fortunes; we are the
authors of our misfortunes.

Let us never feel sorry for ourselves because
of our circumstances. Yes, bad things happen to
good people. Life isn't fair. Never was, never will
be. Yet, a healthy perspective to maintain as we go
through life is to take responsibility for our experiences. Steven Covey said it well. "I am what I
am today because of the choices I made yester-
day." Period, full stop. Additionally, by asking
ourselves, "What am I to learn from it?" we put a
positive spin on the situation. Look for the good.
If we learned something, we have found it. Don't
miss the lesson. Above all, eradicate blame and
the victim consciousness. We cannot simultaneously be the captains of our destinies and the victims of outer circumstances.

Remember, things could *always* be worse. In
our own family, simply remember my brother
Rick, who was hit by a car as he was walking
across the street in the prime of life and was a
quadriplegic for two years before he made his
transition at the age of thirty-eight…or my sister
Susan, who passed away from cancer in her early

forties...or Grandma Gret who watched two husbands and two of her three children pass from the screen of life. And yet she was never bitter, nor did she ever feel sorry for herself. What a great example.

Maybe it was because of these tough experiences that Gret believed that if any problem could be solved with money, it wasn't a big problem.

Whatever problems we may be having at any given time can be dwarfed in a split second if we are suddenly in an accident or cause an accident where someone else is seriously injured or killed. So keep things in perspective and be grateful for what you have.

Do not blame anyone for anything, and specifically don't blame your upbringing for any woe you may be experiencing. I will be the first to admit my many shortcomings and mistakes made. In my efforts to provide you with a spiritual foundation, I let dogma and doctrine take away spontaneity and balance. I am sorry. Find comfort in the fact that I (as did your mom) did the best I could with the resources I had. You have the choice to forgive and heal those hurts or be controlled by them.

All through life, at every moment we have choices. As adults, nothing outside of ourselves controls our life. We make decisions and choices and have to live with the consequences of those choices. As we grow and mature, hopefully we make wiser choices. Many times, the wisest choice is one that simplifies our life.

Feelings are not the cause of our behavior. Don't excuse and justify negative actions because you're feeling a certain way.

We can change negative feelings and a negative attitude by changing our thoughts and more importantly, our actions. What we think is very important and certainly can change behavior, but usually it is one's behavior that changes one's attitude. As O.H. Mowrer puts it, "It is easier to act yourself into a better way of feeling than to feel yourself into a better way of action." In the fourth century b.c., Aristotle said, "We become just by performing just actions, temperate by performing temperate actions, brave by performing brave actions." This concept will be discussed later.

Everyone laughed when the presenter at a workshop said, "Life is all about mind over matter—if you don't mind, it don't matter!" His point was that we have a choice in how we interpret our life experience. We are not our experiences. We are much greater than our experiences, and the quality of our life is largely dependent upon how we see and relate to our experiences. Phil McGraw, Ph.D., commonly known as Dr. Phil, in his bestselling book *Life Strategies*, goes so far as to say that, "There is no reality; only perception." No matter what happens, it is up to us to choose how we are going to interpret the event.

It's not what happens to us, but what we do with what happens to us that matters. Are we going to be angry or forgiving at someone's wrongdoing? Will we chose to be happy for someone's success or be jealous? Will we wallow in self-pity, or see a negative event as a challenge, pull ourselves up by the bootstraps, and make the best of it?

Our viewpoint and analysis of any given situation can obscure how things really are. Human perception is incomplete. We rarely know everything that's going on in any given situation. We compensate by filling in the missing pieces with our own thoughts and beliefs. How we interpret things involves a process of filling in gaps. We don't see what's motivating the harried driver so we assume he is an inconsiderate jerk. Why fill in the gaps with something negative? Maybe the driver is rushing to the hospital or just found out that his wife or child has cancer. Give people the benefit of the doubt.

Be tolerant of other people's mistakes. Many times life is not a rigid black or white, but infinite tones of gray, where we need to be sensitive to people and their human condition. You don't know their circumstances. You have not walked in their moccasins. In another time and place, you could have easily made the same mistake.

All of our choices have consequences. Prior to making a choice, project into the future by asking yourself, "How am I going to feel *after* I do this?"

This can give you valuable information as to whether or not you should make the choice.

Prior to finalizing a decision, try to envision every potential consequence. Look to see the end from the beginning as much as possible.

"Wisdom consists of the anticipation of consequences."

—Norman Cousins

"When making choices, try to narrow the field to three that are acceptable...relying on expert help if you can. Remind yourself that the one you choose doesn't have to be perfect. If it's good enough, it's good enough.

Combat 'decider's regret' by focusing on the good qualities of that which you've chosen and recognizing that even if you had picked something else, you'd still be experiencing some let-down."

—Michael Masterson

꙾ ꙾ ꙾

Don't be fearful to ask for what you want—help, a raise, forgiveness, another chance, referrals (especially referrals!), or whatever. In love and in work, it will award you abundantly.

Nobody is "above" you. Not presidents, CEOs, ministers, movie stars, or models. Don't be intimidated. If God took the time to create you, you have as much value and are as worthy as any soul upon the planet. Your worth has nothing to do with the size of your home, the size of your bank account, or what letters are after your name.

Develop the ability to "fit in" and be compatible with everyone in any setting. Learn to relate to all people at all levels of the socio-economic scale, from a homeless person to the president of the United States and everyone in between.

Be considerate always. Be gracious. Be on time. Say "please" and "thank you" and "you're welcome". Never pull rank. Never be crude or impertinent. Be respectful of other people's time. Never be short-tempered. Don't speak badly about others. Doing so says much more about you than it does about them. Never treat people who have less as less. Build people up. Treat everyone as well as or better than you would like to be treated.

There are "givers" and "takers" in this world. Choose to be a "giver" of love, kindness, support, service, and help. This can be viewed as making "investments"—"investments" that pay dividends. It is far better to have life indebted to you than vice-versa. Maintain balance and self-respect in this giving. Don't over give and become a people pleaser.

We come into this world with a moral intuition of knowing what is right and what is wrong. Listen to it and act accordingly. As Dr. Laura Schlessinger says, simply "do the right thing."

Don't automatically rebel against authority but always question it.

Don't settle. You deserve a happy, fulfilled life. See it, want it, feel it, plan it, take action to get it, and sooner or later it's yours.

March to your own drummer. I've read somewhere that sometimes "majority" only means that all the fools are on the same side.

Humor, more than anything else, gives us the ability to rise above any situation. Try to find humor even in the toughest times. Will whatever is bothering you really matter in a year from now, five years from now? Ask yourself, "What's really important?" Don't take yourself too seriously. Laugh at yourself and you will always have plenty of people to laugh with.

Forgiveness is far more beneficial for you than for the person you are forgiving. Grudges and resentments can rot your life. Let them go. Love is greater than pain. Forgive and return to love. You may have been the one who was wronged this time, but next time it may be you who are in the wrong. Besides, a happy successful life is always the best revenge.

If something *can* be found out, it probably *will* be found out.

Always be reading a book. Henry David Thoreau said, "How many a man has dated a new era in his life from the reading of a book!" Those who don't read are not much better off than those who can't read. Learning from others' perspectives, experience, and wisdom adds a depth and quality and dimension to one's life that can't be attained from just one's own personal experience. Jim Rohn says, "Everything you need for your better future and success has already been written," and this, "...your formal education will make you a living, but your personal education will make you a fortune."

≈ ≈ ≈

Always "default" to the truth. Again from Jim Rohn, "It only takes one lie to taint your testimony."

≈ ≈ ≈

There is always someone to talk to. If you should go through a tough time and need help, know that it is available and go get it. Hire a counselor/coach if you need to.

Certainly don't be too proud to get help. We ask for help not because we are weak, but because we want to remain strong. It is an act of courage. This willingness to seek assistance and new perspectives is admirable. M. Scott Peck says, "The only way that we can be certain that our map of reality is valid is to expose it to the criticism and challenge of other mapmakers...We must constantly revise and extend our understanding to include new knowledge of the larger world."

In this process of constantly revising and extending our understanding to include new knowledge, be certain to pay particular attention to how the world is reacting to you. Are there similar things and responses that happen to you that come from different sources? You're the common denominator with different people and different circumstances. Paying attention to the responses will give you information about yourself. Are personal changes in order? Make them yourself or get assistance, but do something.

At times, we may be tempted to make a pronouncement of something we are going to do. It feels so good, and it rolls off the tongue so easily. Let me tell you something you've heard me say many times: talk is very, very cheap. Unless you are making a public proclamation of something you are going to do as an assurance that "forces" you to do it, because you couldn't live with the embarrassment of not doing it, resist the temptation.

It is far better to do whatever it is you're going to do and then be able to say, "This is what I did."

Benjamin Franklin said, "Well done is better than well said."

And this from Tony Robbins, "...become one of the few who do versus the many who talk."

Every time you say you're going to do something and then you don't do it because of all the good reasons of how life got in the way and prevented you from doing it, your credibility is seriously eroded. And I can assure you there will be times in your life when you need that credibility. At that point, it's too late to go about getting it. You either have it or you don't. Someone is either pregnant or they aren't. Everything you do that reinforces your trustworthiness is like money in the bank. If you tell someone you're going to do something, be damn certain you do it, or don't say it in the first place. A man is only as good as his word.

News commentator and bestselling author Bill O'Reilly relates this concept to respect and success. After stating that he believes success is measured by how many people on this earth respect you, he says, "...gaining respect is pretty difficult. *Always do what you say you are going to do* [emphasis mine]. When you say that you are going to call someone back, you have to call that person back. When you promise to deliver a favor or perform a service, you must come through.... When you discipline yourself to fulfill every one of your commitments—no matter how insignificant—you will be respected…. You have to keep your word and constantly think about the impact you are having on the people with whom you are dealing. You have to *care* [emphasis mine] about that."

So, once again, if you're not absolutely committed to living up to your word, don't say you're going to do something in the first place.

കര കര കര

"The secret of patience…do something else in the meantime."

—Great Quotations Inc.

കര കര കര

In *Hamlet,* Shakespeare said, "To thine own self be true." To that I add: if it's good for you. An example of what I mean would be someone, thinking that to be true to himself and do what he really needed, took heroin or drank a quart of scotch. Not so! In other words, don't house a negative trait or habit in a good-sounding acceptable facade. Life is short. Don't miss the view. Definitely stop and smell the (proverbial and literal) roses. Bring a smile to a child's face. Make a dog's tail wag. Have fun, be happy. Live, love, and laugh much. Don't be afraid to ask yourself, "What do I need to do for me now?" and then do it. Nobody else is going to take care of you. But don't include self-destructive behaviors that ultimately lead to less happiness.

If you're super stressed out, learn to handle it by doing something good for yourself (my first suggestion is exercise). Take a walk or go to a lake or the beach. Too many people do something that is bad for themselves, like eat too much, eat bad food, smoke or drink in excess. The ultimate result of this type of reaction is…*more stress*. Duh, anyone home?

Take quiet time alone.

Life's answers are within us.

Take walks. (The Danish philosopher/theologian Kierkegaard once said, "There is no problem too great that cannot be solved by walking.")

Love nature. Find peace there.

Be it an ocean, a mountain, field, stream, woods, or meadow.

Being in the perfection of nature helps our lives resonate with that perfection.

∽ ∽ ∽

The man whispered, "God, speak to me" and a meadowlark sang. But, the man did not hear.

So, the man yelled, "God, speak to me" and the thunder rolled across the sky. But, the man did not listen.

The man looked around and said, "God, let me see you" and a star shined brightly. But, the man did not notice.

And, the man shouted, "God, show me a miracle" and a life was born. But, the man did not know.

So, the man cried out in despair "Touch me, God" whereupon God reached down and touched the man.

But, the man brushed the butterfly away and walked on.

Don't miss out on a blessing because it isn't packaged in the way that you expect.

—Author unknown

∽ ∽ ∽

Love and respect wild animals, be they ducks, geese, deer, or dolphins.

They fend for themselves.

They individually take full responsibility for their lives and complain not.

And in that responsibility they are wild and they are free.

What a way to live!

In his book entitled *How to Have More than Enough*, Dave Ramsey tells the story of the farmer whose donkey fell into a well. Realizing that there was nothing he could do and that neither the mule nor the well were worth saving, he decided to put the mule out of its misery and fill the well with dirt. When the farmer started shoveling the dirt into the well, the mule became hysterical. As each shovelful of dirt hit his back and fell to the bottom of the well, the mule heed and hawed and whined and squealed. Then suddenly, a thought struck the old mule. He realized that every time a pile of dirt hit him, he could shake it off and then step up on top of it. Eventually the battered, exhausted mule stepped out of the well to freedom. What looked as though it might bury him had actually brought him inch by inch closer to freedom.

In a tough situation, even if we think we have explored every option for resolution, generally there are many solutions that we have not thought of or that have not been revealed to us yet. Maybe it's a timing issue with the universe. Sometimes in "surrendering" the situation to God, the universe, and Infinite Intelligence, the situation will resolve itself or you'll get new perspectives on actions you can take. Point being, just because you haven't thought of a viable solution does not mean there isn't one. There are infinite possibilities. Time is a great revealer.

Sometimes after you have all the facts of a situation, just take the time to "sleep on it." It has been said that sleep is the mother of counsel. Let it all sink in and learn to listen, to trust, and to act on your intuition. What does your "gut" tell you to do?

Following a strong "gut" feeling (differentiated from an emotional want or desire) about something can be wiser and more valuable than continued intellectual analysis. Our bodies have a wisdom of their own, separate from our brains. As a simple experiment, when making a choice of whether or not to make a purchase, tune into and feel your body. Is there a negative (physical) sensation or twinge? Be cognizant and receptive of what your body is telling you. Pay attention to it and act accordingly.

Lynn Robinson is the author of *Compass of the Soul* and *Divine Intuition*. She directs us to ask our intuition open-ended questions like "What's the best way to heal this relationship?" or "What could I do for work that would be fun and profitable?" She says, "Listen for the answers. They'll come through feelings, words, physical sensations, symbols, dreams or just a simple knowing. ...You just have to ask."

"Experience taught me a few things. One is to listen to your gut, no matter how good something sounds on paper."

—*The Art of the Deal* by Donald Trump

Sometimes you can observe a lot by watching...(that's a joke).

Occasionally "unplug" and look at your life as an outside observer, as if you were watching it on television. When we can step apart, eliminate our emotional involvement, and observe, many times we get a better perspective. As you're "watching" the "episode," ask yourself, what did "he" (you) do to get himself into that situation and what are some options for "him" (you) to resolve the situation or to merely move on in a positive direction?

"All the world's a stage, and all the men and women merely players."

—Shakespeare, 1564–1616

≁ ≁ ≁

I once heard your great-grandfather, who we lovingly called PapaArnie, say, "Everything happens for the best."

≁ ≁ ≁

There are either one of two things in life...*results or excuses*. I'm talking about the results you want in a relationship, the results in terms of the body you want, the money you want, the happiness you want, etc. It may seem cold, but it's the truth. There is a time factor that needs to be entered into the equation to get those results, but that does not change the premise…results or excuses.

Everybody dies. It's going to happen to me and it's going to happen to you. The actor Michael Landon, whom I had the privilege to meet, died at a very young age. He was beloved by thousands. He said, "Somebody should tell us, right at the start of our lives, that we are dying. Then we might live life to the limit, every minute of every day." If something you want to do is moral, healthy, and doesn't hurt anyone else…as the Nike ad says, "Just do it."

"In great attempts it is glorious even to fail."

—Vince Lombardi, 1913–1970

"Don't be too timid and squeamish about your actions. All life is an experiment. The more experiments you make, the better."

—Ralph Waldo Emerson, 1803–1882

Be real careful about joining groups. By identifying too closely with any one group, you risk losing your individual perspective and what's really true for you. *Filter everything*, all information (regardless of where or who it is coming from) to see if it is right for you. Obviously, that includes this book. Don't be part of the "sheeple" by doing what your friends, neighbors, or anyone else is doing. Certainly don't compromise your values to be part of the group. What's right for you is the question to ask.

There is an Infinite Intelligence (most refer to it as God) that has created and is running this universe. We are a part of it. It is not *outside* ourselves. There is not someone separate from us that we necessarily need to pray to for gifts or dispensations. We need only to get and stay in sync with this Infinite Intelligence. So, in my opinion, our prayers need only ask that we come into a greater and greater alignment with this magnificent (beyond human comprehension) flow and perfection of life, and to continually express our gratitude for it. Wayne Dyer says that in reality we are "spiritual beings having a human experience." Author Daphne Rose Kingma puts it another way: "Being human is ultimately a journey of spiritual evolution…. We are not just bodies and minds, but souls who have taken on bodies in the human evolutionary adventure we call life…growing, that is our human quest; it's what we're here for…. We are, in fact, eternal spirits who have stepped into life with a grand and specific purpose: to be able to love without limitation."

By the way, don't confuse the doctrines, dogmas, and divisions of religion with any of this. One of my favorite quotes from David Icke is, "God save us from religion."

"A single grateful thought raised to heaven is the most perfect prayer."

—Gotthold Ephraim Lessing, 1729–1781

Many religions convey to their flocks that through their pain and suffering, they are getting "points" in heaven. Obviously, this leads to martyrdom. Surely growth is a welcome outcome of hard times. Benjamin Franklin said, "Those things that hurt, instruct," and David Weed said that "Goliath was the best thing that ever happened to David." We need to face problems directly, work through them, and solve them successfully, learning and growing in the process, and then move on. Be certain not to prolong pain because of martyrdom or false obligation.

"How we see the world creates the world we see."

"What you think about, you bring about."

These are short ways of saying that we are constantly emitting energy on many levels, physical, mental, emotional, and spiritual. This energy that we put out is magnetic in nature, and like a magnet, it will attract more of the same. In *Tao Te Ching*, Lao Tsu writes, "He who does not trust enough will not be trusted." So, be it events, circumstances, people, employers, conditions, things, sickness, or health, we create our world. This brings us back to the theme that runs throughout this book, that we are totally responsible for our lives.

Dr. Phil offers some helpful perspectives, driving home the fact that you are individually responsible for your life. One is the concept of evaluating your behavior in each area of your life by asking the question, "Is what I am doing working?" If there are areas in your life where you are discontent, you are doing something that isn't working and you need to change what you're doing, even if you think what you are doing is right!

Another perspective, which he shares in *Life Strategies*, is the concept that our lives need to be managed and that we are the managers. For purposes of objectivity, he proposes that one think about this manager as if he or she were another person. In the book, he then says to do a performance evaluation on him/her based on the following criteria:

1. Is your life manager keeping you safe and secure from foolish risks?
2. Is your life manager putting you in situations where you can utilize all of your skills and abilities?
3. Is your life manager creating opportunities for you to get what you really want in this life?
4. Is your life manager taking care of your health and well being, physically, mentally, emotionally, and spiritually?

5. Is your life manager selecting and pursuing relationships in which you can be healthy and flourish?
6. Is your life manager requiring you to reach and stretch for those things that will keep you fresh and young and alive?
7. Is your life manager designing your day-to-day flow so that you enjoy some peace and tranquility?
8. Is your life manager arranging for some fun and recreation in your life?
9. Is your life manager structuring your world so that there is balance among those things you consider to be important?"

He asks, "What kind of marks do you give yourself as a life manager? As the evaluator, you may decide that your biggest problem is that you can't fire your life manager.... This is a life manager that you have to work with, motivate, educate and be patient with."

The bottom line is that the quality of our lives is all up to us. We are accountable.

Do the hard stuff in life quickly. Then you can freely enjoy other things without a burden hanging over your head. If you know you have to do something, deal with it, get it over with, and move on to better things. Be careful not to create an excuse of waiting for all outer conditions to be just right before you do what you know you need to do. Those outer conditions may never be what you consider "right." It's a stall, it increases your stress, and ultimately it is only you who is fooled.

Procrastinate later.

~ ~ ~

In Scott Peck's classic book, *The Road Less Traveled*, he defines maturity as the ability to delay gratification. There is tremendous value in this character trait. Don't get fanatical about it, but develop this ability. Start doing it today. You will accomplish your goals and be the receiver of many blessings. He writes, "Delaying gratification is a process of scheduling the pain and pleasure of life in such a way as to enhance the pleasure by meeting and experiencing the pain first and getting it over with. It is the only decent way to live."

~ ~ ~

The self-talk language that we use every day very much defines our experience. For example, call a problem a "challenge" and it takes on an entirely different look and feel. The words we use to describe an event can actually change our emotional experience of that event. Tony Robbins goes into great detail about what he calls "transformational vocabulary." He goes so far as to say that the words that we attach to our experience *become* our experience. Robbins sites two examples. First, he says he and his wife used to get into what they called "pretty intense arguments." They later subsequently described them as "spirited debates," which definitely gives it a different emotional intensity. Spirited debates have different rules than intense arguments. The second example came from Ken Blanchard, when his truck broke down in Africa. He turned to his wife and said, "Well, that's rather *inconvenient*." It worked so well to keep their spirits up; they now use the word on a regular basis. For another example, instead of saying we are mad or angry, if we say we are annoyed or peeved, it lowers the emotional intensity.

Robbins concludes, "Tiny shifts like these change the emotional direction and therefore the quality of our lives."

This is a particularly important point to remember for anyone who describes their life in melodramatic terms, blowing things out of proportion, making a big deal of little things. Unless you're in a profession where dramatization is required, such as a fiction writer, author Richard Carlson reminds us that "Life isn't an emergency."

In the novel entitled *Michelle's Story: The Enlightened Way to Wealth*, one of the characters says, "You'd be a lot less worried about what people think of you...if you realized how *little* they do."

Besides, what other people think of you is none of your business.

Worrying about something does not prevent it from happening. Generally, the things we worry about don't happen. Mark Twain said, "I have been through some terrible things in my life, some of which actually happened." Trust God that you will be okay. Dale Carnegie's worry/stress-busting formula:

1. Live in "day-tight compartments."

2. Ask yourself, "What is the worst thing that can possibly happen?"
3. Prepare to accept the worst by creating a survival plan.
4. Meanwhile, make whatever effort you can to improve the chances that the worst-case scenario won't happen.

❧ ❧ ❧

You need never be afraid, for the universe is a kind and friendly place.

Because you are one with it, it is always on your side, conspiring for your growth and your happiness.

❧ ❧ ❧

Plan and prioritize your days. (Put the top priority items at the top of your list and lower priority items at the bottom. Work from the top.) Jim Rohn says, "Never begin the day until it is finished on paper." Also, be certain you know the difference between *activity* and *productivity* and don't confuse the two. There are excellent time management tools available to assist you with these concepts. Writing down things to do and remember on paper (or electronic format) frees your mind, relieves a tremendous amount of stress, and gives you a sense of control.

Dirk Zeller (*Your 1st Year in Real Estate*) makes an excellent case for doing what needs to be done daily. It's what we do every day that will determine our success. "True success comes from accomplishing daily the activities that will lead you to your ultimate goals in life. Failing to accomplish the daily disciplines will lead you down the path of lost opportunities and lost income." If we got the long-term result *today*, of not accomplishing our daily tasks, we would be much more apt to get done what needs to get done. According to Zeller, "The person who eats fried foods does not pay the penalty at thirty-five; he pays at fifty-five. The person who fails to save 10 percent of his income for retirement is not penalized at age forty, but at sixty. The prospecting we fail to do today does not hurt our income today, but ninety to 120 days from now."

Part of time management is to say no when people try to dump their "monkeys" on you. Don't let other peoples' priorities take over your own. Time is precious. Don't waste it. Regularly ask yourself, "What's the most valuable thing I can be doing right now?" Maybe it's talking with a friend or someone you love. Maybe it's listening to the wind in the trees. Many times, it's reading a book. Seldom, if ever, is it watching TV.

Maybe it's watching a sunset. Maybe it's working on a project, building a business, or establishing a real estate portfolio. Whatever it is for you, if it is getting you closer to your personal goals of happiness, fulfillment, and freedom...it is the right thing to be doing.

In his 20 years of research on tipping behavior, Cornell Professor Michael Lynn says, "The major reason people tip, is to avoid social disapproval." His studies have shown that the quality of service has almost nothing to do with how people tip. Only about 4 percent of the variability in tip size is due to the quality of service. Anyway, tipping experts recommend a 15 percent tip for adequate service, 20 percent for good service and 10 percent for bad service.

If you can't "see" everything that needs to be done, and you don't at the moment have all the answers in any particular situation, take the first step. Many times that's all you really need to do. Generally, this will lead you to step two and so on. St. Francis supposedly said, "Start by doing what's necessary, then what's possible, and suddenly you are doing (what you thought was) the impossible." Simply do the next best thing. Taking control of even the smallest aspect of the problem will overcome the false belief that a problem is all-encompassing. The important point is to *get started now*.

"Do something! Even if it's wrong."

— Orville Richter

"Our grand business is not to see what lies dimly at a distance, but to do what lies clearly at hand."

—Thomas Carlyle, 1795–1881

"Do what you can, with what you have, where you are."

—Theodore Roosevelt, 1858–1919

～～～

Dr. William Glasser describes our behavior as a combination of:

- Thinking
- Acting
- Feeling
- Physiology

We have control over all four aspects of behavior. Over our thoughts and actions the control is direct (believe it or not), and based on the choices we make in thoughts and actions, we have indirect control over our feelings and physiology. His helpful analogy is that we are like the driver of an automobile. The front two tires are our thoughts and actions, and the back two tires are our feelings and physiology. Wherever we steer those front two tires, the back two follow. If you are not happy with the way we are feeling, change your thoughts and actions and your feelings will change.

Identify your feelings. Actually find a word that most accurately describes what you're feeling. This puts you in far greater control. "Nail it" and many times you can trace it backward to where it originated. You can think of feelings like dashboard lights in a car. They are not the source of what's going on, just the indicator that there is something going on. In his bestselling book *Awaken the Giant Within*, Tony Robbins labels feelings as "action signals," and he details what we can learn from them and what actions to take to master them. He explains how we can enjoy the process of learning from all of our emotions.

You have feelings; don't deny any of them, and certainly do not feel guilty for having them. Responsibility and morality are only applicable when you decide to act on what you feel. You are not your feelings. They are neither good nor bad. They just are.

My very good friend and dance partner, Valerie Kratz has been through her share of hard times, having suddenly lost her only son and then her husband within a fourteen month period. Her conclusions about dealing with deep sorrow are insightful. Many times, to truly heal and resolve an unpleasant emotion, she believes that we need to totally immerse ourselves in it and feel it fully. This is a process that may take some time. Although unpleasant, it is sometimes the most direct route to wholeness and to the integrity of our physical, emotional, mental and spiritual alignment. Some people create myriad distractions and pretend certain feelings don't exist. They are cheating themselves of true joy and wholeness because these negative emotions are real and drain life force if not healed.

Contrary to popular belief, Valerie is convinced that time does not heal all wounds. People (the walking wounded) carry around negative emotional issues for decades without ever having any healing taking place. They take emotional traumas from childhood to their graves at the close of a lifetime! No, time does not heal all wounds. It's what we do with the time that will make the difference whether negative emotional issues/traumas are truly healed. So, if you want more joy and peace, deal with stuff sooner rather than later. This healing journey may require spending more time in nature, increased prayer and meditation, educational/inspirational readings and building a support system of friends and family. Sometimes the help of a skilled professional may be necessary. To verify whether an emotional healing has occurred, see if you can recall the causal event without any negative emotional charge.

If we do not impose upon ourselves self-discipline, it will probably be imposed upon us by life. An obvious example is someone who doesn't exercise or take care of his diet and who then needs a heart bypass surgery. Suddenly, he starts watching his diet and starts an exercise program.

Self-discipline can be painful, but in the long run, it is by far easier and a more pleasant choice than the consequence of having it imposed upon us by life. We then do not have the benefit of being in control or really having a choice in the matter. Concerning discipline, Bill O'Reilly says, "The cure for lack of discipline is to learn to make yourself do what you *do not* want to do, and do it *on time*. This is not always easy. But it's worth doing if you want to live comfortable and feel proud of yourself...stay with a project until it's completed.... [This] will make you *indispensable*."

This from Tony Robbins: "Anything you want that's valuable requires that you break through some short-term pain in order to gain long-term pleasure."

This from Jim Rohn: "We must all suffer from one of two pains: the pain of discipline or the pain of regret. The difference is discipline weighs ounces while regret weighs tons."

It is always wise to expend time and money to *prevent* future problems. The energy expended pays back ample returns in a far more peaceful life. Crisis is not fun. Some people live from crisis to crisis. Part of the reason for this is that they don't take the time for preparation and preventive maintenance. The hurdles and pitfalls that can be avoided are many, and the freedom you gain by taking the time to handle stuff ahead of time is well worth the effort. This goes for your health, your car, your home, your relationships, your work, and on and on. Always be *ahead* of the game of life. Dig your well before you are thirsty.

A big part of life is to show up. Show up for opportunities, show up for your responsibilities, and show up for your relationships.

You will be at the right place at the right time.

In martial arts, it is far better to be worthy of a belt you don't have than to have a belt you're not worthy of. The concept is applicable to all areas of life. Your inner accomplishments and who you are is more important than your title or the letters after your name.

A definition of character that I have long believed to be one of the best is as follows:

The ability to stick to a decision long after the initial emotion of that decision is gone.

Here is a perspective on character that was shared with me by Kimberly Lake, someone with impeccable character.

"Reputation comes over one from without; character grows from within. Reputation is what you have when you come to a new community; character is what you have when you go away. Reputation is what men say about you on your tombstone; character is what angels say about you before the throne of God."

Gordon McDonald, in his book *When Men Think Private Thoughts*, defines character in a number of ways. Here are a few of them:

- How a man responds to his enemies and his critics.
- How a man relates to the weak and helpless.
- How a man performs when no one is looking.
- How a man responds to adversity and disappointment.

Character is both developed and revealed by situations.

"Integrity is one of several paths. It distinguishes itself from the others because it is the right path...and the only one upon which you will never get lost."

—M.H. McKee

The results of a study by Robert Half are interesting. Business executives were asked to list the main reasons employees were fired. Seventy percent of those fired in the workplace were fired not because of incompetence, but because of their behavior and their attitude—things like their willingness to work hard, their ability to learn, their strength of character, their persistence, etc.

Competence and skills can be taught—but character, drive, and integrity cannot. They can be learned if the learner is willing to teach himself, but they cannot be taught. (You can lead a horse to water ....)

"If you are not fired with enthusiasm, you will be fired with enthusiasm."

—Vince Lombardi, 1913–1970

Be sensitive and empathetic to the plight of others. Be able to feel and embrace another's hardship as your own and say, "I see your hurt and I'm here to feel it with you. You are not alone."

It is better to be wrong than to be fanatical, and being kind is more important than being right.

"Kindness is the language which the deaf can hear and the blind can see."

—Mark Twain, 1835–1910

The difference between success and mediocrity is not in what we're confronted with, but how we respond to it. It doesn't matter what happens to you, it's what you do with what happens that matters. The quality of your life does not depend on what you encounter, but rather on the person you become as a result. Shit happens. Life is unfair. In his book *Man's Search for Meaning*, Victor E. Frankl documents his life in the concentration camps of World War II. It was an unimaginable hell, and the majority lost hope.

Yet Mr. Frankl became a better, stronger man from his horrendous experience. He documents that he would frequently counsel those who wanted to commit suicide. Quoting from the book, "There was a very strict camp ruling that forbade any efforts to save a man who attempted suicide. It was forbidden, for example, to cut down a man who was trying to hang himself. Therefore, it was all-important to prevent these attempts from occurring." He said that those who wanted to commit suicide would inevitably say that they had nothing more to expect from life. Quoting again, "... it was a question of getting them to realize that life was still expecting something from them; something in the future was expected of them." There is always something more for us to become and to give. Quoting Mr. Frankl one more time, "Whatever we had gone through could still be an asset to us in the future. And I quoted from Nietzsche: 'Was mich nicht umbringt, macht mich starker' (That which does not kill me, makes me stronger)." Hard times and conflict have been described as our spiritual midwife. And our labor is to continuously deliver an improved version of our self to the world. Adversity brings us to the edge of our resourcefulness and helps us give birth to new levels of growth and development.

Robbins says, "Surmounting difficulty is the crucible that forms character."

"If I were asked to give what I consider the single most useful bit of advice for all humanity it would be this: Expect trouble as an inevitable part of life and when it comes, hold your head high, look it squarely in the eye and say, I will be bigger than you. You cannot defeat me."

—Ann Landers, 1918–2002

❧ ❧ ❧

"Things turn out the best for the people who make the best of the way things turn out."

—John Wooden

❧ ❧ ❧

If something is your truth and you're convinced of it, *wear it*. There may be a risk stating it because you may have to either stand alone or stand corrected if your perception is off. This is not easy, but it is important. In his book entitled *Living With Passion*, Peter L. Hirsch says, "When you take a stand, you're going to catch some flak from those people who haven't the courage you do. It comes with the territory.... Speaking of courage, which comes first: having courage and then taking action, or taking action and then drawing courage from it? I'll let Henry Ford answer this one: Courage follows action."

Sometimes, not getting what you want can be a wonderful stroke of luck. Bestselling author Bernie Siegal tells a true story of a man on his way to the airport to catch an important flight when he got a flat tire. It caused him to miss his flight, and he was beside himself with anger. That is until he was subsequently informed that the flight had crashed.

Richard Carlson, in his bestselling book *Don't Sweat the Small Stuff* records the oft-repeated tale that further illustrates this concept. I believe it's worth restating to emphasize the important point that we do not see the full picture at any given time.

There once was a village that had among its people a very wise old man. One day, a farmer from the village went to the wise man and said in a frantic tone, "Wise man, help me, a horrible thing has happened. My ox has died and I have no animal to plow my field! Isn't this the worst thing that could have possibly happened?" The wise man replied, "Maybe so, maybe not." Quite upset, the man criticized the wise man to his neighbors. The very next day, however, a strong, young horse was seen near the man's farm. Because the man had no ox to rely on, he had the idea to catch the horse to replace his ox — and he did. How joyful the farmer was. Plowing the field had never been easier. He went back to the wise man to apologize. "You were right wise man. Losing my ox wasn't the worst thing that could have happened. It was a blessing in disguise! I never would have captured my new horse had that not happened. You must agree that this is the best thing that could have happened." The wise man replied once again, "Maybe so, maybe not." Not again, thought the farmer. Surely the wise man had gone mad.

But, once again, the farmer did not know what was to happen. A few days later, the farmer's son was riding the horse and was thrown off. He broke his leg and would not be able to help with the crop. Oh no, thought the man. Now we will starve to death. Once again, the farmer went to the wise man. This time he said, "How did you know that capturing my horse was not a good thing? You were right again. My son is injured and won't be able to help with the crop. This time I'm sure that this is the worst thing that could have possibly happened. You must agree with me." But, just as he had done before, the wise man calmly looked at the farmer and in a compassionate tone replied once again, "Maybe so, maybe not." The man was enraged that the wise man could be so ignorant.

The next day troops arrived to take every able-bodied man to the war that had just broken out. The farmer's son was the only young man in the village who didn't have to go. He would live, while the others would surely die.

We can all look back at events in our lives that seemed very bad at the time, yet turned out to be a good thing. So take things in stride. Many times there is a higher power that arranges our lives, and we are unable to see the blessing until later. That's why it's so important to pray and strive to be in sync with the Infinite Intelligence that runs the universe. Have faith and remember that the purpose of faith isn't as much about changing a situation as it is about changing our "seeing" of the situation.

    I find it ironic that people who get defensive and are reluctant to admit they were wrong or made a mistake are trying to not look weak, when in reality it is a sign of insecurity and weakness to not admit a mistake. Conversely, it is a sign of strength to admit when you're wrong and be willing to stand corrected. When you realize you've made a mistake, *quickly* admit it and take whatever steps you can take to correct it.

    Recently I was asked what I would do differently if I were suddenly given a billion dollars. After a brief moment of thought, I answered that I would not change a single thing in my life. I would continue writing this book on a daily basis and continue with my goal of becoming a proficient ballroom dancer. Life is good and I am grateful.

Having an attitude of appreciation is so critically important. The Institute of HeartMath (www.heartmath.org) is an outstanding organization that studies the "wisdom" of the heart. In 2004, the U.S. Congress awarded them a $1 million grant to further their studies. HeartMath conducts leading-edge research on the relationship between the heart and brain and the ways in which this relationship affects physical, mental, and emotional health and human performance. Studies have revealed clear positive changes in the nervous system, immune system, hormonal system, brain, and heart when we experience appreciation and other positive emotions. There is *always* so much to be grateful for. Go through life with an attitude of gratitude. While desiring what you want, don't forget to focus on what you have. It will change your whole countenance and attract more blessings for which you can appreciate and be more grateful for. A beautiful cycle.

Melody Beattie says, "Gratitude unlocks the fullness of life. It turns what we have into enough, and more. It turns denial into acceptance, chaos to order, confusion to clarity. It can turn a meal into a feast, a house into a home, a stranger into a friend. Gratitude makes sense of our past, brings peace for today, and creates a vision for tomorrow."

She goes on to quote Collette, a French novelist of the early 1900s, who said, "What a wonderful

life I've had! I only wish I'd realized it sooner."
What a shame to come to this realization late in life.

We all like investments that appreciate in value.
A key to having your life appreciate in value is to
appreciate it more. Think of every day above
ground as a great day.

You can get far more accomplished by consistently doing a little than by inconsistently doing a
lot!

We can always do more than we think we can
do, much more! Maybe it's one more pull up, lap,
or set. Maybe it's one more hour on a project or
one more sales call, whatever. Thomas Edison said,
"If we all did the things we are capable of doing, we
would literally astound ourselves." Most people
fail because they give up much too quickly. It's
good to remember Roger Bannister's four-minute
mile. It hadn't ever been done. Science, sports
medicine, and the whole world said it *couldn't* be
done. Roger Bannister believed he could do it and
he did it. Suddenly, many others started to run

four-minute miles. Today, thousands of runners do it, some even in high school. Why? Because now they *believe* they can do it? Think about it.

"Believe that life is worth living and your belief will create the fact."

—William James, 1842–1910

Affirmations can be a very effective tool to help get what we want. Here are some examples:

- "Every day in every way, I'm getting better and better." (Marc Fisher, *Instant Millionaire*)

- "The Lord hath pleasure in the prosperity of his servant." (Psalm 35:27)

- "Miracle shall follow miracle and wonders shall never cease." (Florence Shinn, *The Game of Life*)

- I live an enchanted life.

- I now attract into my world _____.

Think, feel, and repeat these (or others you like) out loud throughout the day. They make us fallow. It's like adding fertilizer to a garden. Affirmations like these have a magnetic quality that will attract great things.

Having said that, I must give you a quote from Jim Rohn. "Affirmation without discipline is the beginning of delusion."

≈ ≈ ≈

There is no need and no justification to ever say, "It's not my fault" or "I'm sorry, but that's the way I am."

These are handy sayings only if you don't want to grow up.

≈ ≈ ≈

Just as some people are too slow in making a decision, some are too quick. A challenge arises; they panic and think something has to be done immediately without looking at all the options and the consequences of those actions. Any decision made in a highly charged emotional or fearful state is probably a wrong decision.

TO YOUR HEALTH

"The real doctor is the doctor within.
"Most doctors know nothing of this science
and yet it works so well."

—Albert Schweitzer, 1875–1965

"Cutting-edge medical researchers now believe that life and death begin in the digestive tract...diet remains the single most influential factor in overall human health." These are words from a newly released book by Jordan S. Rubin called *The Maker's Diet*. This is a captivating book on health that is based on instruction from the Bible and *The Maker's Diet* may just turn out to be the "Bible" of getting and staying healthy. "History reveals that the healthiest people in the world were generally the most primitive people as well! Our ancestors rarely died from the diet- and lifestyle-related illnesses that kill most modern people before their time, mainly because they ate more healthfully and had more active lifestyles…. Before the arrival of modern agriculture, the human diet of these primitive peoples consisted mostly of fruits, vegetables, wild heirloom grain and seeds, fish, and meat from wild animals. Our bodies *still crave* these ancestral foods, no matter how [much] we 'progress' technologically."

I regret raising you as vegetarians because, from personal experience, I now know that naturally raised beef, chicken, and the other meats written about in Jordan's book are critical for long-term optimum health. Processed food found on grocery store shelves is infinitely more "dead" than animal protein. Jordan makes a clear case that the anthropological data from primitive societies prove that the longest-lived peoples on earth have all been meat eaters. "The stomach's production of hydrochloric acid is unique to meat eaters…. Animal protein is our only complete protein source, providing all eight essential amino acids." Additionally, the only foods containing vitamin B12 that can be metabolized by our body are animal products, especially eggs, fish, red meat, and organ meats.

❧ ❧ ❧

Detoxification is the first step toward vibrant health. Having said that, a very strong immune system, a healthy eliminative system (I'll spare the detail. Just know that this is extremely important), and plenty of nutrients from correct diet and supplements may protect you from everything from the common cold to cancer. Health and healing come from within. This self-healing is possible with a positive mental attitude, good diet, exercise, fasting, plenty of clean water, clean air, and as few pollutants as possible.

❧ ❧ ❧

Illness exists before symptoms appear. View symptoms as the beginning of the cure...as information. It is the language our body uses to tell us that it is upset. According to Guylaine Lanctot, M.D., author of the book *The Medical Mafia*:

"Our reaction, in the face of illness, can be one of two kinds: Either we see it as an enemy, we curse it, and we shut it off with surgery or drugs. We simply negate it. But it will come back knocking at our door, sooner or later. Or, we look upon it as an ally. We rush to decode the message which it has transmitted to us. And we try to resolve the real cause of the problem."

"The beneficial bacteria in the environment and in your gut serve as your first line of immune defense against the unfriendly bacteria and fungi without and within.... Adults and children face even more problems in our toxic world when stress, medications, and poor diet combine to reduce friendly bacteria to such a great extent that unfriendly bacteria begin to thrive."

— *The Maker's Diet* by Jordan Rubin

Examples of important foods that establish friendly bacteria in the gastrointestinal tract are sugar-free yogurt, kefir, and sauerkraut.

Antibiotics indiscriminately kill the good bacteria along with the bad. Don't ever take an antibiotic simply because a doctor says you should. Many times they can be avoided. Weigh the pros and (the many) cons of the decision and you decide.

∽ ∽ ∽

You know how important it was to Gret for you to take good care of your teeth. Get them cleaned regularly. When brushing, concentrate on each tooth separately. Floss daily.

∽ ∽ ∽

Drugs slow down the body's attempts to throw off invading organisms while poisoning the body in other ways. Health is the ultimate high.

∽ ∽ ∽

Most people are starving to death on a full stomach.

∽ ∽ ∽

Take calcium and other nutritional supplements. My readings suggest you consume at least one-half a gram of protein for each pound you weigh and to drink one and one-half to two quarts of water daily. Eat healthy not because you don't want to die but because you want to live fully. Limit carbohydrates. Exercise your body and have an active energetic lifestyle. We were given bodies that thrive on movement. Use it or lose it. Make choices that produce positive results in your body.

If, (God forbid) you find yourself in a position where you need to lose weight, it is as simple as this...burn off more than you take in. You could spend time reading stacks of books on the subject and try many diets, or you can simply burn off more than you take in. Obviously, you need to eat healthy food (and if you do this, you will probably never have the problem) and eat foods that are right for *your* body. The book *Metabolic Typing,* by Wolcott and Fahey, is a fascinating study of how different foods affect each of us. For example, a food that is good for one person may not be good for your body. The book includes a questionnaire to determine each person's metabolic type, what foods to eat, and what foods to stay away from.

Refined sugar is very detrimental. Avoid it! Strive to be so consistent about not eating sugar that when you do eat foods with sugar in them, you can feel good and proud of yourself because it proves you're not fanatical.

⧓ ⧓ ⧓

My personal opinion is that many times emotional issues are as likely to cause a cold as the cold virus itself.

⧓ ⧓ ⧓

Stretch and stay limber. Have strong stomach muscles; it will keep your back healthy. Lift things correctly. Keep your body balanced by strengthening opposing muscle groups. Every minute of sleep before midnight is worth four minutes of sleep after midnight.

⧓ ⧓ ⧓

Only after researching all current information about vaccinations should you make your decision to get or refuse them for you and your children.

Keeping your hands clean prevents sickness. Here is the correct way to wash your hands taken from the Mayo Clinic Web site.

- Wet your hands with warm, running water and apply liquid or clean bar soap. Lather well.
- Rub your hands vigorously together for at least ten to fifteen seconds.
- Scrub all surfaces, including the backs of your hands, wrists, between your fingers, and under your fingernails. (Ninety percent of germs are under fingernails.)
- Rinse well.
- Dry your hands with a clean or disposable towel.

If you're in a public restroom, touch as few things as possible. Leave the water running when you're finished rinsing. After your hands are dry, use a paper towel to turn off the faucet. Then use the same paper towel to turn the doorknob. Usually there is a trash can by the door where you can toss it on your way out.

∽ ∽ ∽

While traveling, wear a seatbelt and if riding with a group, the safest seat is behind the driver.

If you hear someone yell fire or you smell smoke, and you need to open a door to escape, feel the door to see if it is hot before you open it. If you do open it, open it from a crouched position and be ready to crawl out if there is smoke because smoke usually rises and the oxygen is near the floor.

∽ ∽ ∽

Please practice safe, loving sex and if it meets those criteria, may you practice plentifully.

∽ ∽ ∽

The author would write about relaxing, but he doesn't know anything about it. His readings do indicate though, that there is an overwhelming consensus of opinion that it is definitely a good thing to do from time to time. He's working on it.

❧ ❧ ❧

Thanks go to Dr. Mercola's e-newsletter for finding the following humorous quotes, which were taken from actual medical records, as dictated by physicians.

- Patient has two teenage children, but no other abnormalities.
- Skin somewhat pale but present. She stated that she had been constipated for most of her life until she got a divorce.
- Rectal examination revealed a normal-size thyroid.
- Occasional, constant, infrequent headaches.
- By the time he was admitted, his rapid heart had stopped, and he was feeling better.
- The patient has been depressed ever since she began seeing me in 1983.
- The patient is tearful and crying constantly. She also appears to be depressed.
- The patient refused an autopsy.
- The patient has no past history of suicides.
- Between you and me, we ought to be able to get this lady pregnant.

RELATIONSHIPS ARE PARAMOUNT

"The future of relationships is moving us toward the vaulting awareness of who we really are as human beings, something we have managed to avoid for a very long time by being so thoroughly committed to convention.... This is the future of love—vast love, love beyond boundaries, love without preconceptions and judgments, love without outdated myths ...."

—Daphne Rose Kingma

The Future of Love, written by Daphne Rose Kingma, is a powerful ground-breaking book on love and relationships. Neale Donald Walsch, the author of the bestselling *Conversations with God* books has placed *The Future of Love* on his list of "Top Ten Books That Can Change the World."

In her refreshing, highly endorsed book, Kingma dismantles our previous assumptions about what form our relationships have and shows us that a higher love isn't concerned with form nearly as much as with content. The soul, which she describes as the divine fragment within us, "... isn't interested in marriage—or any other relationship for that matter—except as it allows a person to become more aware of his or her own soul."

Her captivating, easy-to-read book beautifully articulates that the purpose of all of our myriad relationships is to increase our soul's capacity for love. She says, "The soul is shifting our relationship focus from form to content, from rigidity to flexibility, from containment to expansiveness, from our emotional needs to real love."

Relationships are to heal, change, and transform us into something more.

Treat people as if you or they had six months to live. Be concerned for what their memory of you will be. They may not always remember exactly what you said or what you did, but they will recall how you made them feel. If you want to be immortal, love someone. You will live in their heart long after you are gone. Create good memories with those you love.

Remember that the greatest gift you can give someone is your time.

"People are unreasonable, illogical, and self-centered. Love them anyway. If you do good, people will accuse you of selfish ulterior motives. Do good anyway. If you are successful, you will win false friends and true enemies. Succeed anyway. Honesty and frankness make you vulnerable. Be honest and frank anyway."

—Unknown

"Love is life.... And if you miss love, you miss life."

—Leo Buscaglia, 1924–1998

"We're all looking for more love. It's that simple. In the end, nothing else really matters."

—Daphne Rose Kingma

Dr. Glasser's philosophy says that to accomplish any goal, ask and answer these questions. (WDWP might be a way for you to remember it.)

- What do I *want*?
- What am I *doing* to get it?
- Is it *working*?
- What's the *plan*?

Although this applies to all areas of life, this was put in the relationship section to remind us that there needs to be goals set in this area. Many times folks think of setting goals in areas of health, finances, or a project, yet relationships are the most important thing in life, so goals here are important.

Guide yourself in your interactions with adults (especially those you love) by asking yourself, "Will what I am about to do, bring me closer to this person or move us further apart?" On the flip side of that though, be careful that your actions are not totally dictated by how you think they are going to make someone else feel. A balance is needed. We need to be kind and respectful of others while maintaining our self-respect and addressing our individual needs. If we believe that we should not do something for ourselves, fearing that it might hurt someone we care for, then whenever we meet our own needs, we'll feel guilty. We are responsible for what we do, not for how others feel in response to what we do. Conversely, we are responsible for how we feel regarding other people's actions.

∽ ∽ ∽

"Any fool can criticize, condemn, and complain—and most fools do."

—Dale Carnegie, 1888-1955

It is not pleasant to be around people who are negative, complain, criticize, or blame. Don't be one of these people. In his *New York Times* bestseller, *Don't Worry, Make Money*, Richard Carlson, Ph.D., says that it is extremely common for struggling individuals to continually blame someone or something for their lack of joy and abundance. Conversely, it is extremely rare to find a successful person who whines, complains, and frets about his or her circumstances. He says, "The real question is: What came first—the attitude or the success? The answer, in virtually all cases, is that the winning, positive attitude came first, followed by a lifetime of abundance."

Don't get stuck on "what isn't." We think things *should* be this way or that way and on and on it goes. Instead of being negative and complaining about what's happening in our world, we need to accept "what is" at any given time. Learn from it and certainly, if we're not happy with "what is," start taking steps to improve the situation. But if we are totally preoccupied with how we think things should be, we are probably missing the lesson being presented in "what is." This, in turn, prolongs the undesirable situation or prevents us from seeing that actually looking from another vantage point, it is a blessing in disguise.

Be understanding, tolerant, and adaptable, but don't compensate for and enable someone's weakness. Don't be fooled into thinking that it is the kind, responsible thing to do. You do them a great disservice and they will end up resenting you. You are not getting any bonus or brownie points from God! If you keep rescuing a person from their misery they have created by their own actions, that person will never learn to be responsible. So kindly speak the truth as you see it, and let the chips fall where they may.

We need to set our boundaries, learn to say no sometimes, and let them know that we are not going to be a caretaker or take on a false responsibility for their life. This will help them grow up. In her bestselling book *Codependent No More*, Melody Beattie writes, "Caretakers look so responsible, but we aren't. We don't assume responsibility for our highest responsibility—ourselves. We consistently give more than we receive, then feel abused and neglected because of it." When someone is having a problem, instead of saying, "Here, let me do that for you," we need to learn to say, "I'm sorry you're having that problem. What do you need from me?" You are not responsible for anyone else's happiness.

In her excellent book *Divorce Busting*, author Michele Weiner-Davis clearly details that changing yourself and how you act and respond to a significant other can definitely change a relationship. But don't believe that simply loving someone enough will change them. Also, don't be fooled into thinking that becoming a better person will change someone else (except maybe your children). This is codependent behavior. By all means, always strive to become a better person; don't count on it changing anyone else. You cannot change, control, nor fix anyone. It is futile to try. In any situation, you can only change you. You can only control you.

Another aspect of codependent behavior is described by author Gary Simmons in his book, *The I of the Storm*. Quoting from his work, "Codependence places the burden of one's well being on the performance of someone else. When conflict arises...the tendency is for the dependent person to blame the other for their disappointment or upset." Not good. So, be neither dependent nor codependent. Author Stuart Wilde says, "Design your life so that you don't require things from others. Try to need only those things you can get yourself." When that's not possible, Beattie says, it's acceptable to "... ask people for what we need and want from them because this is part of taking care of ourselves and being a responsible human being."

When you're giving of your time, going out of your way, performing favors for someone, don't assume they know that and will be therefore grateful or "keeping track" of what you're doing for them. If you think they are and they aren't, down the proverbial road, the chances of major resentments forming are great. Unless resolved, this will end up hurting the relationship big-time. So your original intent of building the relationship by doing things for someone backfires and the exact opposite happens. Now…to avoid this rather unfortunate series of events, simply let the person know that you value the relationship and because of that, you are going out of your way, doing something that you'd really rather not be doing or doing them a favor. It is quite okay to do this. It will trigger an appreciative response that is good for both of you. And if it doesn't, you now have information to maybe make some decisions of who to do favors for in the future.

Not that you need their approval, but when contemplating a mate, you might ask yourself, "Is this person someone I'd be proud to introduce to Mom or Dad?" Additionally, when choosing a life mate, here is an analogy worth considering. It comes from my attorney friend, Kirk Rogers. Imagine you and your partner playing tennis together, both on the same side. The tennis balls that keep coming over the net are life's ups and downs, the many never-ending challenges of living on planet Earth. Then, simply ask yourself, "Is this the person I want as my partner in this game of life?"

True love is not just an overwhelming feeling, *it is a decision.* In her excellent article entitled "Recognizing Unconditional Love," Dinah S. Temple defines different types of love. Useful information.

Infatuation is temporary love, an object of extravagant short-lived passion.

Conditional love is loving *if* someone acts a certain way.

Reasonable, logical love is based on someone loving another because he or she has a certain characteristic or fulfills a need of the other person.

Unconditional love is based on someone loving another in spite of what has come to pass or what may come in the future. It is love with no strings attached. It is love without restriction, reservations, or conditions. It is the ability to maintain pure love in spite of all odds or circumstances.

It may be common sense, but I think it's worth saying that when choosing a mate, seek someone who hasn't had too much trauma in his or her life, or be quite certain the person has really worked through it. Find someone who does not have big areas in life that are unresolved. A big plus is if they have a good relationship with their parents and are complete and happy with themselves. Working through your own unresolved issues will certainly help you attract this type of person. Weiner-Davis says, "Although loving someone can be one of life's most gratifying experiences, it must be the icing on the cake. In the same way that eyeglasses sharpen images as opposed to giving vision to the blind, you must be whole in order to feel whole with your mate…unless your life has definition and meaning without your mate, your relationship is doomed from the start."

Your relationship with a significant other is always a process. You never really "get there." It's a process of learning and loving and growing that is always moving and in a state of flux. Learn to love the process. All diamonds have flaws and as Confucius says, "Better a diamond with a flaw than a pebble without."

Never cheat on your mate. If you find yourself in a relationship that you are not happy in, you might want to try counseling, books, seminars, etc. to remedy the situation. If nothing works, muster the courage to be honest and handle it without a third person getting involved. Allowing a third person in to end a relationship is the coward's way out.

Did you hear the one about the couple in their nineties who filed for divorce? They were asked why, after being married over seventy years, they were getting a divorce. Their reply: "We wanted to wait until the children were dead."

If you feel you need to end a relationship or if someone is ending a relationship with you, play your part in kindness, gratitude, and love. Daphne Rose Kingma says, "Indeed, what an incredible leap in our evolution it would be if we could both fall in love and break up in love—with tears of thanks, with generosity.... The truth is that wherever love has once existed, it remains...any coming together with another soul has been a gift of spirit ..."

Be grateful for the growth you've experienced and the good times you have shared. Certainly don't discount the pleasant times you have had simply because you're not going to have more. Move on in peace and with an excitement of what awaits you.

Speaking to the author here, don't avoid problems to keep the peace. Lack of conflict doesn't mean there are no problems. Neither does it solve them.

"Life would be easy...if it weren't for other people."

—The comic title of Connie Podesta's video series

Whenever you go out on a date (or any time you go to someone's home), always bring a gift of some kind. It doesn't have to be expensive. Maybe just pick a flower, but don't show up empty-handed. Additionally, don't just *think* compliments. When someone looks good or is kind or generous or warm or intelligent, or you like the way their house is decorated, etc...say it! Tell them!

If you're having a meal at someone's home, volunteer to wash the dishes, clean the kitchen or empty the trash. If you're a guest for an extended stay, remember the saying that house guests are like fish...in three days they start to smell. In addition to being neat and orderly, volunteer to help with their chores. Water the lawn, weed the garden, clean out the gutters, whatever. Leave the house cleaner than when you arrived. Keep in mind that when visiting, you are the one on vacation with the free time; your host isn't, so it is incumbent upon you to conform to their life schedule.

It has been said that we either speak out our feelings or we act them out. Buried emotions are not buried dead; they remain alive to trouble us.

In an authentic relationship, many times you need to communicate your feelings even though you may think that it may be divisive. If you want to tell somebody that it bothers you when they do something, you may be tempted to believe that it would be better not to mention it because the relationship will be more peaceful (classic for me). So you keep it inside. But sometimes in that effort to keep the peace, the relationship is compromised.

In his book *Why Am I Afraid To Tell You Who I Am?* bestselling author John Powell speaks of how essential emotional openness and honesty is with a significant other. He calls it "gut-level" communication. One of the rules for gut-level communication that he reports is that there must be no judgment coming from either person. He says, "… I realize that I cannot judge the intention or motivation of another. I must be humble and sane enough to bow before the complexity and mystery of a human being. If I judge you, I have only revealed my own immaturity and ineptness…. Emotional candor as such does not ever imply a judgment of you…. For example, if I were to say to you, 'I am ill at ease with you,' I have been emotionally honest and at the same time have not implied in the least that it is your fault that I am ill at ease with you. Perhaps it is my own inferiority complex…" or my indigestion!

William Glasser, M.D., gives an example of how to successfully communicate a problem someone has with their mate in his book *Staying Together*. "If the problem is not enough affection, a common cause of marital dissatisfaction, I suggest that the dissatisfied partner say, 'I have a problem with the fact that there is not enough affection—kind words, hugs, kisses—in our relationship. I want you to help me figure out what I (not you!) can do to bring more affection into our lives.' This is not criticism because it is not demanding that the other do anything different."

All of this is not to say that we need to act out or communicate whatever we are feeling when we are feeling it. We all have a choice as to how we are going to behave. We can feel one way and chose to act another. And sometimes it may be wise to do just that. For example, if we feel anger, we don't necessarily need to say we're angry or yell or walk out. By acting out your anger at that moment, you risk saying or doing something you'll later regret. Obviously one option is to see how you feel later when you are more clearheaded. Feelings don't cause actions. We chose how to act. So, author Weiner-Davis advises that in relationships, "While being able to say what's on your mind is an extremely valuable skill, true assertiveness entails picking and choosing the important battles, not having a knee-jerk reaction to every provocative situation."

The process of how conflicts are resolved is a critical component of a successful, loving, intimate relationship. It's essential that you are with someone you feel very safe to be with, where you don't have to plan every detail of how you're going to say something. Instead, there is a love and a trust where issues can be explored together (from the same side of the table) without judgment or the fear that what you say will be used against you. Seek understanding of the other person's behavior. People who feel they are *understood* will almost certainly feel that they are loved. Both partners need to approach conflict with an openness to learn, not to defend. The goal in a committed relationship should be not what's right for either one of you, but what's right for the relationship. Being open and vulnerable creates intimacy. As Drs. Jordan and Margaret Paul state in their book entitled *Do I Have to Give Up Me To Be Loved By You?* "… it is not the resolution of conflict that creates intimacy as much as the process of getting there."

Even in the midst of a very intimate relationship, the genuine lover always perceives the beloved as someone who is totally separate. This

separateness and uniqueness needs to be encour-
aged. We need to cherish our individual freedom
and not restrict the freedom of our partner. The
prophet Kahlil Gibran speaks of this freedom:

But let there be spaces in your together-
ness,
And let the winds of the heavens dance
between you.
Love one another, but make not a bond of
love:
Let it rather be a moving sea between the
shores of your souls ...
Sing and dance together and be joyous, but
let each one of you be alone,
Even as the strings of a lute are alone
though they quiver with the same music ...
And stand together yet not too near together:
For the pillars of the temple stand apart,
And the oak tree and the cypress grow not in
each other's shadow.

Being a friend with your mate is a critical
component of a successful relationship.

Sometimes we treat our friends better than we treat our mate! Generally, we don't criticize or try to control or change our best friends. We listen, love, and support them. World-renowned psychiatrist/author William Glasser, M.D., claims that in a romantic relationship, even if friendship is preceded by love and sex, "If friendship is not quickly and firmly established, love soon withers." Continuing on this theme that friendship is the key to a good long-term relationship, he states, "The more interests a couple shares, the better the chances that their marriage won't go stale and they won't start living separate intellectual lives…. Friendship is based on sharing common interests, being able to say what's on your mind without fear of rejection or criticism, planning and building a life together, and most of all looking forward to being with each other when there is nothing pressing to do…. Someone you can talk with anytime about anything is the ultimate in marital friendship." A successful loving relationship always contains an element of ongoing mutual psychotherapy.

Henry David Thoreau said, "Could a greater miracle take place than for us to look through each other's eyes for an instant?"

The ability to be objective in any given situation is definitely something worth developing. Not getting defensive and putting yourself in the other person's shoes to see and feel the situation from their perspective will be recognized as a sign of maturity, and it will be respected as the antithesis of self-centeredness. This objectivity will most definitely enhance the quality of your relationships.

Author Richard Carlson conveys one aspect of objectivity when he advises us to replace a knee-jerk defensive response to criticism with mere acceptance. He says, "… there are many times when simply agreeing with criticism defuses the situation, satisfies a person's need to express a point of view, offers you a chance to learn something about yourself by seeing a grain of truth in another position, and, perhaps most important, provides you an opportunity to remain calm…. Give this strategy a try…you'll discover that agreeing with an occasional criticism has more value than it costs."

ç┐ ç┐ ç┐

Groucho Marx said, "I don't care to belong to a club that accepts people like me as members." Then there was the lady who stood up in one of Phil Laut's seminars while he was talking about self-esteem and said, "You know, the only problem with going on vacation is that I have to take myself along."

Wherever you go, there you are. You will be with yourself for the rest of your life.

Love yourself and if there are parts of you that you're not happy with, change them. How can we expect others (particularly a significant other) to love us if we can't even love us? In his book *People of the Lie*, M. Scott Peck writes, "As psychological adults, we have all learned to a greater or lesser degree that in order to be loved, it is our responsibility to make ourselves lovable." Rather than seeking to be loved "... when we nurture ourselves and others without a primary concern of finding reward, then we will have become lovable, and the reward of being loved...will find us."

Certainly don't sacrifice who you are for your mate, but always analyze what you can change and what you can do to make them happier. If it's the right mate, they will be doing the same thing. Attention and caring are very different from sacrifice and martyrdom. There is great pleasure in doing what our partner wants us to do. Whether a relationship is having problems or not (particularly if it's having problems), don't be afraid to ask your mate how you can be a better partner. You get the information and then you make the choice if you can fulfill their wishes.

Drs. Jordan and Margaret Paul state, we will give freely only when we feel we can say, "No, I really don't want to do that for you …," and not be punished. We do not really enjoy saying yes unless we feel the freedom to say no. Only then can we give out of caring, rather than out of fear, duty, or guilt.

MAY YOU PROSPER

"Nothing in the world can take the place of persistence. Talent will not; nothing is more common than unsuccessful people with talent. Genius will not; unrewarded genius is almost a proverb. Education will not; the world is full of educated derelicts. Persistence and determination alone are omnipotent."

—Calvin Coolidge, 1872–1933

The first whack on a boulder by a stone cutter produces no result, not even a scratch. Maybe the first one hundred or one thousand hits produce nothing. Then with one hit, the boulder splits in two. Was it just the last hit that broke open the rock? Hardly. It was all the previous blows that

97

were necessary. So just because you are not see-ing immediate results, it does not mean you're not making progress. Learn to love the process and the results will come.

It has been said that the process of attaining abundance is all about having a big enough "why." If your reason to acquire abundance is big enough and strong enough, the "how" will pres-ent itself, and you will have the persistence to accomplish your dream. It's called leverage. Ever notice how much you can get done in the two days before leaving on a vacation? It's because you had a strong "why." What if you could always be that productive? If you or your child's life depended upon you making $100,000 in the next year, you'd probably find a way to make it hap-pen.

For many, simply the ability to buy things becomes secondary to the desire to be free—free from worrying about money. Whether it's worry-ing about the ability to pay your bills or worrying whether or not you will be able to buy whatever you need. Can you feel how exhilarating it would be to not have any financial stress? Can you feel the sense of freedom and independence that gives you?

We can't be totally free if we're not financially free. In his excellent book, *The Trick to Money Is Having Some*, Stuart Wilde says, "You are trying to become a truly independent being—abundance is one aspect of that independence...just making money for the sake of making it *can* become vapid and boring, but when your financial success is linked to your spiritual desire for true independence, then your money-making efforts take on a kind of holiness."

Your health is the ultimate wealth, and your relationships are more important than money. Don't sacrifice either for money, although money can enhance both your health and your relationships. Without it the tail wags the dog.

Mark Fisher and Marc Allen, in their excellent book *How to Think Like a Millionaire*, say that it is obvious that your situation will not improve if you do nothing about it. But hold on! It is not obvious to many people. How many people are there that go through life desiring a better financial future but do nothing more to improve their lives financially other than to buy lottery tickets and wish?

"Success is a result of backbone, not wishbone."

—Anonymous

In their book they say, "Just as the source of true happiness lies within each of us, success also comes from within. Success is the result of a very specific mental attitude."

We need to develop that mental attitude. Tony Robbins says that one of the most important beliefs to adopt is the belief that in order to succeed and be happy, we've got to be constantly growing and improving the quality of our lives. He encapsulated the concept with a mnemonic that he created and trademarked as CANI! (pronounced kuhn-EYE). It stands for Constant And Never-ending Improvement. It relates not only to business success but to every aspect of our lives.

Whether it be through reading books, listening to tapes, attending seminars, or talking with successful people, etc., we will be much happier if we adopt the mental attitude of CANI!

I took a break from writing this chapter to read Robert Kiyosaki's book called *Rich Dad Poor Dad*. You need to get the financial education in that book that you unfortunately did not get from me or from school. You need to get a deep understanding of what the difference is between an asset (something that puts money in your pocket) and a liability (something that takes money out of your pocket). You will be surprised. I will include some quotes from the book, but I strongly recommend that the very next book you read after this one be *Rich Dad Poor Dad*.

You can either make money or make excuses. Successful people do what unsuccessful people refuse to do. Action is the key and massive action equals massive results. General George S. Patton referenced taking action by saying, "A good plan violently executed right now is far better than a perfect plan executed next week." But action won't happen until you realize that you are responsible for your success. Tell yourself the following truths.

"My parents owe me nothing."

"My children owe me nothing."

"My friends owe me nothing."

"The world owes me nothing."

Although they are not easy to find, seek out sources of income that are residual in nature. In the classic book *The Richest Man in Babylon*, written in 1926, George Clason writes, "I tell you my students, a man's wealth is not in the coins he carries in his purse; it is the income he buildeth, the golden stream that continually floweth into his purse and keepeth it always bulging. That is what every man desireth. That is what thou, each one of thee desireth; an income that continueth to come whether thou work or travel."

Income streams exist where you can do something once and get paid on it over and over again. All assets, as defined by Kiyosaki, certainly do this, and there are some professions that do this as well. Dramatic examples include successful authors or musicians who keep getting paid over and over based on their previous work. More common examples might be an insurance agent who gets paid every time his client renews their policy or network marketing where you get paid on repeat sales from the same customers.

It's good to remember the cliché, "What goes around, comes around." Ralph Waldo Emerson articulated the concept when he wrote, "The sower may mistake and sow his peas crookedly; the peas make no mistake, but come up and show his line." We create our own experience.

According to Larry Winget, author of *Money Stuff*, there are four attitudes about money that need to be totally accepted and believed before we can experience abundance, attract riches, and simply have more money. Here they are:

1. Money is a good thing.
2. You deserve all the money you need in order to have the things you want.
3. There is enough money in the world for everyone to have plenty.

4. Having plenty of money really can happen to you.

If you bullshit your way through a situation, about 90 percent of the time the other person knows it...but you don't know they know it. Stick to the truth and don't stretch it too much.

"After eating an entire bull, a mountain lion felt so good he started roaring. He kept it up until a hunter came along and shot him. The moral: When you're full of bull, keep your mouth shut."

—Will Rogers, 1888–1935

Cars are a terrible investment. Don't buy them new (a new car loses about 25 percent of its value the moment you drive it off the lot), and avoid payments if at all possible.

It's not *who's* right, it's *what's* right that matters. Keep your ego out of the situation.

Some avoid making decisions because of the
fear that if they are wrong they will be held
accountable. Don't be overly concerned about
this. Life is about making choices and decisions
and learning from them. Robbins says, "… there
are no failures in life. There are only results. If
you didn't get the results you wanted, learn from
this experience so that you have references about
how to make better decisions in the future." And
this from Stuart Wilde, "The name of the game is
to see your defeats as seminars you paid to attend
to learn the game of life." And this summation
from Will Rogers: "Good judgment comes from
experience, and a lot of that comes from bad
judgment."

"Failure is success if we learn from it."

—Malcolm S. Forbes, 1919–1990

Give freely to worthy causes. Ten percent is good. This is important. It primes the pump. It demonstrates to yourself and the universe that you are not fearful but confident and optimistic of future abundance. This prosperity conscious-ness will attract prosperity. If you feel you are lacking something, give it away. Whatever it may be, money, a smile, love, etc., this law of reci-procity works, but only when you give to give, not to get.

"The more we give, the more we have."

—Daphne Rose Kingma

Decide what you want. Calculate the approx-imate price you have to pay to get it (there is *always* a price to pay for anything we want to attain in life), and then...resolve to pay the price. Maybe the price is fourteen-hour work days for a while. Maybe it's sleeping at the job for a while. Whatever. We can have anything we want if we have a burning desire and are willing to pay the price. When the going gets tough, the tough get going. Never give up. Kiyosaki says we create our own luck. Everything is within our reach.

Balance is good, but many times, particularly at the beginning, *focus* is more important than balance.

In his book, *Create Your Own Future,* Brian Tracy says that the most successful CEOs in the world, work on average 59 hours per week. "This amounts to either six 10-hour days or five 12-hour days," he says. "In my many years of studying successful people, I have never found a person who has achieved anything worthwhile working the basic eight hours per day. Your success in competitive business will be in direct proportion to the number of hours that you work in addition to eight each day, and over 40 hours per week."

After deciding what we want, Stewart Wilde says to, "… cut out everything from your life that is not a part of the plan. That allows you the power, clarity, and focus to empower just your plan. By getting rid of the attachments and confusions you make your plan important. To succeed it is vital that all of your ducks be heading in the same direction."

"Success usually comes to those who are too busy to be looking for it."

—Henry David Thoreau, 1817–1862

Money magazine recently conducted a study on ten things that make people happy. Here are four that are particularly important to me.

1. *Stay organized.* They report that people who can generally find what they need quickly are happier than those who can't. Concerning paper, all through your life you will be handling papers. Put them in a file folder, label it, and file it in alphabetical order. This greatly increases your chances of finding what you're looking for.

2. *Pay bills as they come in.* Don't let them pile up. It's far less overwhelming doing it in bits and pieces.

3. *Save at least 5 percent of your income.* They showed that people who regularly save money, even if it is a small amount, are much happier. To do this successfully you must pay yourself first. This is one of the main tenants in *The Richest Man in Babylon.* Clason writes, "… 'necessary expenses' will always grow to equal our incomes unless *we protest to the contrary* [emphasis mine]." Don't turn a "want" into a "need" simply because you have the money to buy it. As soon as you get money, make it "disappear" into protected accounts. According to *The Millionaire Next Door,* by Stanley and Danko, millionaires invest a minimum of 15 percent of their income and they "…

create an artificial economic environment of scarcity for themselves and the other members of their household."

"It is the money we save, not the money we make, that determines our wealth...every time you are confronted with an opportunity to spend, ask yourself: Will this make me richer in the future?"

—Michael Masterson

"If you know how to spend less than you get, you have the philosopher's stone.... Beware of little expenses. A small leak will sink a great ship.... Ere you consult your fancy, consult your purse."

—Benjamin Franklin, 1706–1790

4. *If you have credit cards, pay them off every month.* Nobody can afford the high interest charges. It is my opinion that if you are in debt, you are enslaved.

"One of the cardinal rules of credit: Use credit only to buy assets that will appreciate, such as real estate; never use credit to buy depreciating assets, such as cars, furniture, vacations, and electronics."

—*Millionaire Real Estate Mentor*, by Russ Whitney

"Having debt is mentally draining and financially expensive. It makes you subordinate to others, subject to their whims, unable to tell your boss to 'shove it,' and incapable of having a good night's sleep. You don't need to be in debt to live the good life. You need to borrow money for a house, but that's about it. Going into debt for cars and clothing and fun is just plain stupid."

—Michael Masterson

"As the person who has health is young, so the person who owes nothing is rich."

—Proverb

"What can be added to the happiness of a man who is in health, out of debt, and has a clear conscience."

—Adam Smith, 1723–1790

"What are three words that profile the afflu-
ent? FRUGAL FRUGAL FRUGAL."

— *The Millionaire Next Door*, by Stanley
and Danko

ᵔᵔ ᵔᵔ ᵔᵔ

Although it is possible to work for someone
else and make plenty of money, the statistics
show that the chances are slim. Jim Rohn says
that, "Profits are better than wages. Wages make
you a living, profits make you a fortune." In their
excellent book, *The One-Minute Millionaire*, Mark
Victor Hanson (of the Chicken Soup books
fame) and Robert Allen say that "... there are
only four ways to become a millionaire:

1. Investments
2. Real Estate
3. Business
4. Internet

"...The world is desperate to have more
entrepreneurs. According to Warren Buffett,
there are only two ways to create wealth: find
value or create value. Entrepreneurs find and create massive value for other people at a profit.

Entrepreneurs create jobs, foster excitement, and basically make the system work. They see possibilities where others see only problems. Entrepreneurs think to grow rich. As they do, they inevitably enrich the lives of others."

"Destiny is not a matter of chance; it is a matter of choice. It is not something to be waited for; but rather something to be achieved."

—William Jennings Bryan, 1860–1925

Be open to, seek, and create business opportunities. When starting a business, have experienced people advise you, and concentrate your attention on what really matters. What really matters is sales and cash flow. What's your best product or service? What is the price? How are you going to market it? All other details, like setting up the office or bookkeeping, etc., are secondary. There really is no other reason to be in business except to collect and count the money.

"... The only paycheck that is truly secure is the one you create for yourself."

—Russ Whitney

Quoting again from *The One-Minute Millionaire*, Mark Victor Hanson and Robert Allen also recommend some right-brain activity for your business. They recommend "applying the principles of attraction to *envision* perfect customers easily flocking to your doors on a regular basis."

No one can reach their full potential alone. The correct other people give you leverage, which according to Hanson and Allen is critical. They talk about using other people's money, experience, ideas, time, and work in the business world to get leverage and how you can network your way to riches. "Networkers develop and nurture contacts for information, support, advice, referrals, and resource utilization as well as to reach out and connect with whoever they want, whenever they want.... Your network creates your net worth, because at some level, all business is done through people." Seek out influential people you respect and collect business cards, names, addresses, and phone numbers of all the people you meet along the way. Develop relationships with people *before* you need something from them. If you do this, they will be much more receptive to your requests.

Hanson and Allen tell of a study conducted in the late 1960s by Stanley Milgram. The result was known as the "Six Degrees of Separation," which means that through our social networks, all of us are within six connections to anyone on the planet!

Whatever it is you may need, start asking people if they have the information or knowledge. If they don't, ask them if they know anyone who does. It is amazing what connections can be made utilizing human resources.

The bigger your network, the bigger your net worth. Make the effort to cultivate connections. The old adage is still quite true...your success is far less dependent on *what* you know than on *who* you know.

According to *The Millionaire Next Door*, by Stanley and Danko, "... self-employed people make up less than 20 percent of the workers in America but account for 66 percent of the millionaires." If you're working for someone else, you're building *their* dream. Your employer did not go into business to build your dream. When you're working for someone else, you're trading your precious time for money. Lesson #1 in Kiyosaki's book is that the rich don't work for money. He distinguishes between one's profession, e.g., teacher, banker, doctor, etc., and one's business...those actions that are moving one toward financial independence (increasing your assets). Kiyosaki sites that McDonald's founder Ray Kroc was clear about this distinction. He writes that after speaking to the MBA class at the University of Texas, Kroc asked the students, "What business do you think I'm in?" The expected answer was forthcoming. "Ray, who in world does not know that you're in the hamburger business?" To which Mr. Kroc responded by saying, "Ladies and gentlemen, I'm not in the hamburger business. My business is real estate." He knew his *profession* was selling hamburger franchises, but that his *business* was the accumulation of income-producing real estate. So, while you're going about your profession, simultaneously be increasing your financial intelligence. As Kiyosaki puts it, "mind your own business" by increasing your income-producing assets.

Also, if you're working for someone else, it is so very easy to get raises and go up in the ranks. Simply work harder and smarter than everyone else. Do things with excellence. Go the extra mile. Do more than what you're asked or expected to do. Take on more responsibility. Treat your employer's business as if it were your own. If you're reporting a problem, think of possible solutions that you can report at the same time. If you can show them how they can increase their profits, reduce their costs, or expand their customer base, you will be invaluable to them. Heck, if you do that, you might end up being president or owning the company.

New positions always open up (sometimes you can even create your own), and you will stand out like a polished diamond in your employer's mind. You've already proven yourself worthy of the new position giving you more responsibility because you have chosen to take on more responsibility in the past. A key to promotion is to become the new position before it is offered and it will eventually be offered.

Information from the Early to Rise newsletter (www.earlytorise.com) says, "Like it or not, appearance counts. Probably more than you imagine. When you are in a competitive world—and achieving success anywhere is competitive—why give yourself the handicap of a bad appearance?"

Career coach Barbara Reinhold writes on the employment Web site, Monster.com: "Studies have proven that people who are considered attractive are more likely to get hired and be promoted, independent of their performance."

And this from author Michael Masterson: "You can't dress sloppily and expect to be thought of as orderly and respectful inside. You dress rudely or crudely because you think it's OK to do so. Thinking it's OK to dress that way says something about you." What we need to do is simple and inexpensive. To eliminate the risk of the judgments of others that may very well hamper our progress, doing these simple things will demonstrate that you are a high-quality person.

- Keep your hair clean and well cut.
- Keep your body clean and odor free.
- Keep your nails trimmed.
- Dress in good clothes only (even when they are casual).
- Stand and sit with good posture.
- Walk proudly.
- Smile generously.

"It's no coincidence that the words *poor* and *slob* are often linked."

—Michael Masterson

"The way we dress says a lot about us before we ever say a word.... Don't put up unnecessary hurdles for yourself. Make it easy for people to take you seriously."

—Donald Trump

☙☙☙

If you are in sales, do not fear rejection. Courage has been described as being afraid and doing it anyway. The people are not rejecting you personally. It's all in the numbers. Talk to lots of people every day. If you are new to the profession, what you lack in skills you can make up in numbers. Don't give up.

"The best way to deal with rejection is to get as much as you can as soon as you can to reduce its effect on you."

—Dirk Zeller

☙☙☙

If you're in a management position, always try to hire people that are smarter than you (Donald Trump's philosophy is to hire the best from the competitors). Always *ask* them to do what needs to be done, as opposed to telling them (not that they have an option to say no unless they want to find other employment). Treat your employees with a tremendous amount of respect and recognize their accomplishments. Catch them doing something right. Take the time every day to connect with each employee you are in contact with. If they like you (although remember that your primary responsibility is the success of the business, not to make friends) and respect you, they will be far more productive, which will make you look good. They will be doing it for *you* and not just for a paycheck. Zig Ziglar says that the five most important words are "You did a good job." The four most important words are "Can I help you?" The three most important words are "Would you please?" The two most important words are "Thank you." And the single most important word is "You."

If you are in the corporate world, here is some political advice from *Early to Rise*. "… When working in a corporate environment, it's always been my policy to:

"1. Give my boss more value than he has a right to expect, and

"2. Let him know whenever I do something good.

"If you aren't doing these things in your work life, maybe you should. You don't have to be a braggadocio to get the word out. You need only be brave enough to start a conversation.

"One good idea recommended in *How to Become CEO*, by Jeffery J. Fox, is to try to get involved in projects that are important, visible, or 'the pet projects of senior people.' If you don't already know what those projects are, you can find out by simply asking. Ask your boss. Ask your boss's colleagues. Ask your company's CEO, CFO, or whoever. Identify two or three such problems and then choose one that you'd be interested in working on. Present yourself to the person in charge of dealing with that problem and offer to help in any way possible. Don't be pushy. Be enthusiastic. And don't be demanding. Be obliging, almost servile.

"To establish a company-wide reputation for being an up-and-comer, you need two or three large feathers in your cap. You'll get one feather for each such voluntary effort. As you go about putting in these extra hours, be sure to document them with casual memos to everyone possible. Be discrete, but be ubiquitous.

"One caveat: Try never to claim more than is just. In fact, try not to boast about your successes at all. You can get the word out merely by talking about them to the people that count. Ask for their opinions. Share ideas that might be helpful to them. Get into the mix. Let the key people know how good you are without seeming to want them to know ..."

Additional advice for those in the corporate environment comes from authors Lorraine Dusky and Betty Lehan Harragan. Quoting from an article entitled "10 Rules of the Work World," they state:

"1. Rank has its privileges. There is no way you can leapfrog, bypass, overrule, ignore, challenge, disobey or criticize your boss and not get penalized in the game.

"You may disagree with your boss privately, correct some misconception, or even fill her in on some technical detail in your area of expertise, but not in public. No matter if the boss says something that's not accurate or even outright wrong. For your purposes, he/she is right. Absolutely, finally, and positively.

"2. Hard work is not enough. Success isn't that simple anymore. Attitude, image, initiative, confidence—a handful of intangibles—plus how well you do your job are what give one person the winning edge over another.

"3. You were hired not just to do the job but to make your boss look good. Suppose you're the manager of the information-systems department and you devise a way to do an audit better, faster, easier. Your method will save time and money. Now, do you tout your fantastic solution, making sure everyone knows that your boss had nothing to do with it? Or do you bring your boss on board, ask for any suggestions to improve the program, and together sell the solution to the higher-ups?

"Assuming your boss isn't a thief who wants to take credit for others' ideas and work, sharing the glory usually increases your own.

"4. You have to be a team player. One day, you've got the ball; another day, someone else is running with it. If you can't or won't help others achieve their objectives, your colleagues won't be there for you either. It's not just higher-ups who can sabotage you; your peers can make or break your projects.

"5. Thick skins protect soft souls. You can expect that every driving, successful boss will have times when his patience is thin. So let the fast and furious comments roll off your back. Remind yourself that everybody is working together to get the best possible job done. Don't be a doormat, but don't get crazy when some-body snaps.

"6. Information is crucial. To do your job well, you need to know who gets along with whom, who once got along with whom but does-n't now, and why. Learning the history of rela-tionships in your office can save you considerable embarrassment.

"7. A positive attitude brings positive feed-back. Unless you're enthusiastic, you are going to have a hard time getting ahead. Low morale can kill a career as fast as you can say, 'I hate this assignment.' The right attitude may differ from place to place, but if you don't have a positive outlook, it will reflect in your work and things will only go downhill. If you really hate a place, do yourself a favor and get out.

"8. Total honesty is for your shrink. 'Although candor and emotional honesty can be valuable assets in personal relations, letting it all hang out in a work setting can be unwise, inappropriate, and often damaging,' Janice LaRouche writes in *Strategies for Women at Work*. You especially do not want to involve your superiors in your personal life—nor do they want to be involved (no matter how understanding they seem when you recite your tales of woe).

"9. Work friendships are usually transitory. People come and go in an office. They get pro-moted over you or you might get promoted over them, or they go to work for somebody you have declared an enemy, or what's worse, someone you have declared an enemy may become your boss. So think of your friendships at work as alliances related to a specific task, which is what they are, no matter how genuine they seem to be during the job. Don't expect the alliances to be permanent.

"10. Sometimes, you have to ignore the rules. Sometimes, you will make a lifelong friend at the office and the relationship will be hassle-free. Sometimes, you will marry the boss's daughter. Sometimes, it could cost your company millions because the boss is making an egregious error at a meeting with a vendor or a client and you're the only one with enough guts to speak up and correct him. Sometimes, you have to go over your boss's head, your boss's boss is impressed, the boss gets fired, and you get the job. The point is, these rules are general guidelines, not absolutes. But before you break any of them, consider your company's culture, your boss, your own job— and have a good reason.

"Knowing the rules won't guarantee that you'll rise to the top, but at least you won't set up roadblocks for yourself along the way. Corporate politics is a game, first and foremost. Failure to play by the rules will almost always result in your being sidelined, no matter how good you are at your work."

❦ ❦ ❦

Generally speaking, it would be a waste of time and resources to get in our car and start driving with no idea of where we are going. The same is true of our lives. Dave Ramsey says, "The truth is, many people do not have a vision for their lives. They don't expect to go anywhere or to do anything significant in life, so they make few plans and even less preparations. They are the floaters. Laid back on their rubber rafts, they are floating out to sea. Without a vision or a direction, they are content to be controlled by the whims of the water and the wind. Naively, they are enjoying what they think is a free ride, oblivious to the fact that they are vulnerable to every violent change in the weather." Mark Fisher says that, "Almost all successful people started achieving their dreams only when they set clear goals and time plans for meeting them…. We achieve what we plan to achieve, no more, no less." Don't forget that *action* is the key. Tony Robbins says to never leave the scene of a decision without taking some action to accomplish the goal of the decision.

"One hundred percent of the shots you don't take don't go in."

—Wayne Gretzky, Canadian ice hockey player

To assist in having the vision to set your goals, ask the right questions. The size of the question determines the size of the answer. For example, Mark Victor Hanson says, "If you ask yourself 'How do I earn or create a million dollars?' your mind goes to work to discover the answer.... Note that most individuals ask themselves questions like these: 'How do I get a job, salary, or work? Or 'Can I earn $50,000 doing this?' The wrong question will generate the wrong result or a less-than-outstanding outcome."

Examples of wrong questions are, "Why me?" or "What's the use?" or "Why do these things keep happening to me?" Not only is it a victim mentality, but worse yet, our minds go to work to answer the questions with answers like, "Because you're stupid or because it is your lot in life." It totally perpetuates a negative condition.

Tony Robbins goes into great detail about the power of questions in his seminars and says that, "Quality questions create a quality life." He tells a story of a friend of his named W. Mitchell who had two-thirds of his body severely burned and then years later was in an airplane accident where he lost the use of his legs and was confined to a wheelchair. Yet the questions W. Mitchell asked were questions like, "How can I use this?" "Because of this, what will I be able to contribute to others?" "What do I still have?" and "What am I capable of now, even more so than before?" Robbins continues with the story: "After his airplane accident, while in the hospital and paralyzed from the waist down, he met an incredibly attractive woman, a nurse named Annie. With his entire face burned off, his body paralyzed from the waist down, he had the audacity to ask: 'How could I get a date with her?' His buddies said, 'You're insane, you're deluding yourself.' But a year and a half later, he and Annie were in a relationship, and today, she's his wife. That's the beauty of asking empowering questions: they bring us an irreplaceable resource: answers and solutions."

Thinking big is a key to large profits. As an example, Richard Carlson sites successful insurance salespersons who insist that it takes the identical amount of time to speak to someone about a million-dollar policy as it does about a one-thousand-dollar policy. Another example might be a real estate agent listing a $500,000 home as opposed to a $100,000 home. It takes the same amount of time. The bigger your vision the larger your potential for success.

You've probably heard that there are three kinds of people in this world.
1. Those who make things happen
2. Those who watch what happens
3. Those who say, "What happened?"
We each decide in what group we're in.

In the bestselling book *The Millionaire Next Door*, the authors identified what they felt were the seven common denominators among successful wealth builders. Three of these "millionaire secrets" are:
1. They live below their means (the one *fundamental* rule of wealth building).
2. They allocate their time, energy, and money efficiently, in ways conducive to building wealth.

3. They believe that financial independence is more important than displaying high social status.

Have as a goal multiple income streams, so if one is unexpectedly cut off, you're not faced with a dire emergency. Additionally, have enough available saved money to live for at least six months. Napoleon Hill said, "...Without money, one must take what is offered, and be glad of it." And, as a side note, while we're on the subject of being prepared, I highly urge you to have stored food and an alternative water source. The less self-sufficient we are, the more dependent we are on the system, the government, and other people, a vulnerable position you don't want to be in. The more self-sufficient we are, the freer we are.

Many of us have heard the oft quoted definition of insanity which is…continually doing the same thing and expecting a different result. Get comfortable stepping out of your comfort zone. There are great rewards in those unchartered waters. In our quest for financial independence, if we have a "whatever it takes" attitude, the attitude that says we will do anything to accomplish our goal, we're halfway there. Most times it is the bold rather than the brilliant who accomplish financial freedom. Fortune favors the brave.

Remember that success is a continuing journey and not a destination. Learn to love and focus on the process. Don't be overly attached to the outcome. Tom Landry, former coach of the Dallas Cowboys, illustrated this point when he said that his job was to teach the players to run, kick, pass, catch, block, and tackle, and the score would take care of itself. Nonattachment to the outcome has the added benefit of taking the pressure off. You win regardless of the outcome.

Concerning business deals, author Stuart Wilde, in his excellent metaphysical book *Silent Power*, says, "When you are desperate for a deal, you push it away or you wind up paying more. By having little emotion and letting others know that you can walk at any time you become strong. Before every deal, take a moment in the hallway to remind yourself that you don't need it. If you don't get it, it doesn't bother you. If you do get it, it will be under your terms, and you won't pay too much."

Donald Trump, certainly one of the most successful dealmakers in the country, sees a deal from both sides, structures it so it is a win/win situation, and then convinces the other guy it's in his interest to make the deal. Additionally, he always goes into a deal anticipating the worst. He figures that if you plan for and can live with the worst, the good will take care of itself. His exact quote is, "Protect the downside and the upside will take care of itself."

You need somewhere to put the money you are saving. Although I haven't been a big stock market fan, statistically over the decades, it has been a good investment. Lynn Carpenter, editor of the "Fleet Street Letter," reveals that the secret of Warren Buffett's legendary success is what she calls "thinking little." She counsels to not bet on the high-risk, triple-digit returns until you have a solid base of reliable earners in your portfolio.

Carpenter says to find undervalued companies with:

- excellent fundamentals
- sound business models
- a significant marketplace advantage that will carry them to higher earnings in the future

Once you've established that foundation, you can speculatively invest in the big gainers with the hope and expectation of very high returns.

Be truly happy for other people's success. It does not mean there is less for you. In fact, according to Richard Carlson, "... as people achieve their goals, the pie gets even bigger for the rest of us.... We can all succeed and each time someone does—anyone—it helps the rest of us." The universe is an infinitely abundant place and there's plenty of prosperity for everyone. Remember also that anything someone else can accomplish, you can accomplish if you desire it enough. And don't just *try*, but actually *take the necessary action* to attain it. Maybe you remember the sign I had in my office with big bold red letters that said, Make It Happen!

"Luke, you either do, or you do not—there is no 'try.'"

—Jedi Master Yoda, *Star Wars*

As we shouldn't get jealous of other people's success, so too we should help other people not get jealous of our success. The Early to Rise newsletter gives some information to make it easier for others not to feel jealous or envious. "Don't talk too much about your success. Don't, for example, talk about awards you've won, famous people you've met, or how much money you've made.

"If the subject comes up, make a concerted effort to diminish your own role and praise others.

"Eschew…the trappings of success—the fancy cars, the expensive watches, anything that's ostentatious.

"Most importantly, be interested in other people—in what they are doing and what successes they are having. Focus attention away from yourself, even while you work on achieving more of your own goals."

Tony Robbins says that most people's lives are a direct reflection of their peer groups. I have read that our income is the average income of our ten closest friends. We want to surround ourselves with quality people, and there are wonderful people in every economic category. Obviously, don't choose friends simply based on their cash flow, but having said that, it is not wrong to seek friends that have lots of money...certainly not to get their money, but to get their knowledge. Charles Givens, the author of *Wealth Without Risk*, has said, "If you want to learn about money, learn from someone who has a lot of it." There is unanimous agreement among success writers that finding and working with a mentor is critical for notable success. There is a Chinese proverb that says, "A single conversation across the table with a wise man is worth a month's study of books."

"The people with whom we surround ourselves have a great deal to do with what we become."

—Michael Masterson

᛫ ᛫ ᛫

"A hundred years from now it will not matter what my bank account was, the sort of house I lived in, or the kind of car I drove.... But the world may be different because I was important in the life of a child."

—widely distributed poster

When we think of people like Gandhi or Mother Teresa, we realize the tremendous impact one person can have on the world. But what we may not realize is that these famous people may owe much of their success to some unnamed, unknown teacher or parent or friend who influenced them. Many times, making a difference is more important than making money. And many times you can make *more* of a difference if you have money. Some say to measure sales in dollars and success in service. Marianne Williamson says, "A person acting from a motivation of contribution and service rises to such a level of moral authority that worldly success is a natural result." Great thought, don't know if it's true.

The person asking the questions in a conversation is the person that is in control of the conversation. It is easy to develop rapport with people by asking them questions about themselves. Ask about their family, their occupation, where they live and how long they've lived there, what they do for recreation, what brings them to wherever you are, etc. People generally like talking about themselves. Take a genuine interest in what they are telling you. Make a point to remember their name by rhyming (Paul is tall; Shirley's hair is curly; Stanley is manly), by imaging (picture Peter standing on top of St. Peter's Cathedral), and/or by using their name repeatedly in the conversation. Certainly don't respond in conversation with the intent to impress people. It sets up a competitive atmosphere and is irritating. People don't care how much you know until they know how much you care. The ability to establish rapport with great numbers of people will give you a tremendous advantage in accomplishing your goals.

You will be introducing people your whole life. It's good to know how to do it properly.
1. Say the name of the senior person first. This is the higher-ranking or older person.
2. Provide a bit of information about each person to help them springboard into a

conversation. For example, "Jane Doe, this is John Smith, our new staff member. Jane Doe is our CFO."

Concerning your handshake when being introduced or greeting someone, grip firmly and warmly, without squeezing hard. Look them in the eyes. Compliment them if it's appropriate, and if you're complimented, simply say thank you.

Additionally, develop the habit of extending your hand and introducing yourself.

Don't impulsively spend money just because you have it. Save money, learn how to make it grow, manage it wisely, and more will come to you to manage. Money is more important than things. You can always acquire things with money. The reverse is not true. Generally, people who view money as income to spend are people who may have lots of things but are probably deep in debt. Jim Rohn says, "The rich invest their money and spend what is left; the poor spend their money and invest what is left."

If we want the freedom that money provides, it should be viewed as something to save and invest rather than income to spend. Financial independence trumps material showmanship every time.

Those with the most options have the greatest control of their lives and are the happiest of people. Although money doesn't necessarily bring happiness it definitely increases one's options. And there's this perspective from Groucho Marx: "Money frees you from doing things you dislike. Since I dislike doing nearly everything, money is handy."

From the Early to Rise newsletter comes this information. The benefit of a positive outlook is that you feel good and this is obviously very important. But feeling good and achieving your goals are two different things. Self-made people are pragmatic and pragmatic people don't count on luck. They count on action. "Success in life is the result of specific physical actions. You make a phone call. You write a sales letter. You build a restaurant. If the physical actions make sense…if they are the right actions…you will succeed. If they do not make sense, you will fail…if you want to succeed, develop a pattern of behavior that leads to success."

"… getting wealthy doesn't depend as much on whether you are a positive person or a negative one as it does on the specific actions you take, or fail to take, to build your wealth …."

Continuing to quote the *Early to Rise* newsletter, it lists some traits one needs to become successful.

To become successful you must …

1. Take responsibility for the current condition of your life. If you don't have what you want, it's nobody's fault but yours. Figure out what you want and set a specific goal—one that benefits not only you but also others.

2. Write the goal and create a written logical plan to achieve that goal.

3. Learn whatever you need to know to complete your tasks.

4. Focus on the most important tasks (not the urgent tasks) and do them first.

5. Work hard at least fifty hours a week—following your plan. Have a "whatever it takes" attitude.

6. Always focus on solutions, not problems. "What do I need to do right now to make this better?"

7. Develop a network to help you. Do this via phone calls, e-mails, and personal notes. Use that network whenever you can.

8. If and when you feel like giving up and are ready to quit, work one more day.

If you can do these things, you will surely succeed. And your success may be greater and come faster than you expect.

In an article called "Your Hour-a-Day Fast Track to Success", author David Galland tells of a simple, tried and proven method that he says will work for just about anyone. He says, study something for one hour a day in the same way that a college student would study one of his courses. "This is a concept that was popularized by Earl Nightingale a half-century ago and then largely forgotten. But, as Nightingale discovered, daily study is a trait of almost all successful individuals. And it quickly pays off…in just six months of concentrated, one-hour-a-day study, you can understand the basics of almost any topic.

"… Happy with the company you're already working for? There is no surer way to move up the corporate ladder than by learning more about the industry you're in. After just a month or two of daily study, you'll be demonstrating your fast-growing knowledge on the job and attracting the attention of your superiors.

"During my first real job as an office boy in a convention-planning firm I stumbled across Nightingale's hour-a-day idea. After that, I made it a practice to stay in the office for an hour or two after everyone else went home in order to learn the convention business. In just over a year, I was the executive vice president of the company and the boss of everyone else in the office: six employees, all of whom were significantly older than I was.

"In less than two years, I owned 25 percent of the company simply because, aside from the president, I was the only one who knew how to actually run a large convention from beginning to end.

"… There are many careers for which that minimal effort will get you well on your way. How long, for example, would it take for you to become a really competent video editor? To learn how to build a great surfboard? To learn the critical principles of design for Web sites?

"Regardless of what you choose to study, don't procrastinate. If you don't learn something new today, you will just be one day older and not one bit smarter tomorrow."

"God's gift to you is more talent and ability than you could possibly use in a lifetime. Your gift to God is to develop as much of that talent and ability as you can in this lifetime."

—*The Science of Getting Rich*, by Wallace Wattles

POTPOURRI

"If people knew how hard I worked to get my mastery, it wouldn't seem so wonderful after all."

—Michelangelo, 1475-1563

Self-made millionaire Michael Masterson claims that it takes one thousand hours of study to learn a complex subject and five thousand hours to achieve mastery. The bottom line is that it takes a lot of effort to get good at anything. The NFL teams spend fifty times as many hours practicing and preparing for games than on the games themselves.

"Repetition is the mother of skill."

—Tony Robbins

Striving to imbue our every act with excellence gives our lives a certain spiritual quality. And if, as Stewart Wilde says, "… you can perform a function well, you not only have the pleasure of knowing that you're damn good at what you do but also you will eventually have a niche in the marketplace from which you can never be moved." So always do your best and have the self-discipline to put in the necessary time to attain mastery.

Look what it did for Michelangelo.

"The difference between the number one PGA tour player, Tiger Woods, and number 150 is about one stroke per eighteen holes and over $4 million in earnings."

—Your First Year in Real Estate, by Dirk Zeller

ᖾ ᖾ ᖾ

Of the thousands of quotes that I have read, there has been only one that has ended up framed on my wall. It is attributed to Theodore Roosevelt.

"Far better it is to dare mighty things, to win glorious triumphs, even though checkered with failure, than to take rank with those poor spirits who neither enjoy much nor suffer much, because they live in that gray twilight that knows not victory nor defeat."

Over a century ago, Thoreau observed that "the mass of men lead lives of quiet desperation."

Will Rogers said, "The taxpayers are sending congressmen on expensive trips abroad. It might be worth it except they keep coming back!"

I'll spare you many pages of what I could write on the stark contrast between what government is today and what it was originally intended to be. For the moment, suffice it say that unfortunately, government is not your friend. Here's a quote from Ayn Rand. "… it cannot be repeated too often that the Constitution is a limitation on the government, not on private individuals—that it does not prescribe the conduct of private indi-

viduals, only the conduct of the government—
that it is not a charter for government power, but
a charter of the citizen's protection against the
government."

"It is dangerous to be right when the government is wrong."

—Voltaire, 1694–1778

Seldom, if ever, pay retail prices. With all the
discount stores, Web sites, and upscale consign-
ment stores there are, it's silly to pay full price for
anything. National retail chains like Banana
Republic and others regularly rotate their stock
to discount tables. You can also go to the store's
Web site and check out their clearance section.
Richard Carlson reminds us that everything is
used the day after we buy it and suggests pur-
chasing some things used. It's better to purchase
fewer high-quality items than many cheap items,
and sometimes we can find high-quality items
that are used for a good value.

Better to have one hundred guilty people go free than have one innocent person denied his freedom.

Analogies are very useful in conveying a concept and even valuable in establishing a philosophy of life. Using a dance as an analogy to life, writer Bob Sehlinger says, "Like life, a dance has a beginning and an end. But unlike a journey, your objective is not to get to the end, but to enjoy the dance while the music plays." We adjust our steps and movements to the music. It's been said that life may not be the party we hoped for, but while we are here we might as well dance.

Another analogy to life is sailing. You have no control of the wind, but regardless of what direction it is blowing, by adjusting the sails properly you can arrive at any destination. In a card game analogy to life, it is simply a matter of playing the hand you're dealt. Whatever of these or other analogies you like best, the point is that we have control over our actions and responses to life. I believe it was Dale Carnigie who said if we are given lemons, we have the choice to make lemonade.

❦ ❦ ❦

Public speaking and death are said to be people's greatest fears, with public speaking being the greatest. I think it good to do some public speaking to overcome this fear. I recommend joining Toastmasters International for a period of time. They usually meet in small groups, are very supportive, provide excellent informal training, and give you the opportunity to practice. I have listed below some of their suggestions if you are to give a speech to a group of people.

1. Know the room. Be familiar with the place in which you will speak. Arrive early, walk around the speaking area, and practice using the microphone and any visual aids.

2. Know the audience. Greet some of the people as they arrive. It's easier to speak to a group of friends than to a group of strangers.

3. Know your material. If you're not familiar with your material or are uncomfortable with it, your nervousness will increase. Practice your speech and revise it if necessary.

4. Visualize yourself giving your speech. Imagine yourself speaking—your voice loud, clear, and assured. When you picture yourself as successful, you will be successful.

5. Realize that people want you to succeed. Audiences want you to be interesting, stimulat-

ing, informative, and entertaining. They don't want you to fail.

6. Don't apologize. If you mention your nervousness or apologize for any problems you think you have with your speech, you may be calling the audience's attention to something they hadn't noticed.

7. Concentrate on the message—not the medium. Focus your attention away from your own anxieties and outward toward your message and your audience. Your nervousness will dissipate.

By far the most important piece of advice in the above list is to know your material. Most nervousness comes from the fear that you're going to mess up. If you're totally confident in your subject, you'll never have this problem.

Jim Rohn agrees that knowing your material through extensive preparation is essential and yet concludes with this quote. "Effective communication is 20 percent what you know and 80 percent how you feel about what you know."

Of course, don't forget the oldest rule in speechmaking. At the beginning of your presentation, tell them what you're going to tell them…then tell it to them…and finally at the end, tell them what you just told them.

And then there's my personal favorite, the three Bs. Be brief, be sincere, and be seated.

◦◦◦◦◦

In his writings, Stuart Wilde speaks of becoming a strong confident person. He says, "I know it's hard to exude confidence if you don't feel completely solid. But you can fake it 'til you make it. Just by...*controlling your emotional reactions, you dominate your psychology.* You act out a silent strength even though you may not be resonating it deeply within as yet." (Emphasis added.)

◦◦◦◦◦

On a personal note, I have chosen my careers based on two things in this order of priority. First, where I felt I can make the most money and second, where I can simultaneously have the most freedom. If there is potential of significant money to be earned, temporarily giving up freedom (to focus intensely) with the hope that the amount earned will give me freedom in the not too distant future is no problem. As long as I don't really hate the work, the project is moral (robbing banks is definitely out), and it provides a benefit to people, it doesn't too much matter to me what the project is.

I'm all for following your passion, but not to the poorhouse. Staples founder Thomas Stemberg does not believe in following your passion. He bluntly has said, "I think following your passion is a really dumb idea. I follow a great market that provides an opportunity to satisfy customers and to make money."

That's not to say that we shouldn't identify our talents and then find out how to use them to make money. By all means, we need to do this. We all have unique talents and abilities that only we can deliver. If we can incorporate our talent into a creative idea for a product or service that the public will want to buy from us, we can become wealthy. Additionally, if you can turn your hobby or lifelong dream into a way to earn a good living, by all means, do so. But, after your research, if there is no good business idea to support it, forget it.

Michael Gurian, the author of the book *The Good Son*, says that the measure of a man is in developing the following characteristics: decency, fairness, empathy, self-sacrifice, respect, loyalty, service, responsibility, honesty, and honor.

"No legacy is so rich as honesty."

—William Shakespeare, 1564-1616

Edited from the Internet...What I've Learned
- I've learned that you should always leave loved ones with loving words. It may be the last time you see them.
- I've learned that you can keep going long after you think you can't.
- I've learned that we are responsible for what we do, no matter how we feel.
- I've learned that either you control your attitude or it controls you.
- I've learned that heroes are the people who do what has to be done when it needs to be done, regardless of the consequences.
- I've learned that sometimes when I'm angry I have the right to be angry, but that doesn't give me the right to be cruel.
- I've learned that just because someone doesn't love you the way you want them to doesn't mean they don't love you with all they have.
- I've learned that maturity has more to do with what types of experiences you've had

and what you've learned from them and less to do with how many birthdays you've celebrated.

- I've learned that no matter how bad your heart is broken, the world doesn't stop for your grief.
- I've learned that our background and circumstances may have influenced who we are, but we are responsible for who we become.
- I've learned that two people can look at the exact same thing and see something totally different.
- I've learned that credentials on the wall do not make you a decent human being.

∽ ∽ ∽

In my readings I came across a commencement speech given by Anna Quindlen to a graduating class at Villanova University. I think it worthwhile to quote it in part.

"... Get a life. A real life, not a manic pursuit of the next promotion, the bigger paycheck, the larger house. Do you think you'd care so very much about those things if you blew an aneurysm one afternoon, or found a lump in your breast?

"Get a life in which you notice the smell of saltwater pushing itself on a breeze over Seaside Heights, a life in which you stop and watch how a red-tailed hawk circles over the water or the way a baby scowls with concentration when she tries to pick up a Cheerio with her thumb and first finger. Get a life in which you are not alone.

"Find people you love and who love you. And remember that love is not leisure, it is work. Pick up the phone. Send an e-mail. Write a letter. Get a life in which you are generous. And realize that life is the best thing ever, and that you have no business taking it for granted.

"Care so deeply about its goodness that you want to spread it around. Take money you would have spent on beers and give it to charity. Work in a soup kitchen. Be a big brother or sister. All of you want to do well. But if you do not do good too, then doing well will never be enough.

"It is so easy to waste our lives, our days, our hours, our minutes. It is so easy to take for granted the color of our kid's eyes, the way the melody in a symphony rises and falls and disappears and rises again. It is so easy to exist instead of to live.

"… I learned to love the journey, not the destination. I learned that it is not a dress rehearsal, and that today is the only guarantee you get. I learned to look at all the good in the world and try to give some of it back…and I tried to do that, in part, by telling others what I had learned. By telling them this:

"Consider the lilies of the field. Look at the fuzz on a baby's ear. Read in the backyard with the sun on your face. Learn to be happy. And think of life as a terminal illness, because if you do, you will live it with joy and passion as it ought to be lived."

The following has gone around the Internet many times, but I feel it is worth repeating here.

- If you find yourself stuck in traffic, don't despair. There are people in this world for whom driving is an unheard of privilege.
- Should you have a bad day at work, think of the man who has been out of work for years.
- Should you despair over a relationship gone bad, think of the person who has never known what it's like to love and be loved in return.
- Should you grieve the passing of another weekend, think of the woman in dire straits, working twelve hours a day, seven days a week, to feed her children.

- Should your car break down, leaving you miles away from assistance, think of the paraplegic who would love the opportunity to take that walk.
- Should you notice a new gray hair in the mirror, think of the cancer patient in chemotherapy who wishes she had hair to examine.
- Should you find yourself at a loss and pondering what is life all about, asking "what is my purpose?" be thankful. There are those who didn't live long enough to get the opportunity.
- Should you find yourself the victim of other people's bitterness, ignorance, smallness, or insecurities, remember, things could be worse...you could be them!

Of all the people I have ever met or known, your Great Uncle Orv, in my opinion, provides the greatest example of how one should live. There certainly are richer men in the world, but there are none that are as wealthy. While the rest of the world was planning their lives and trying to make more and more money, Orv was living his life and living his dream. He is a man of honor, truth, and sincerity. He is a man of action, of self-confidence, courage, and generosity. His priorities are straight. The good will and joy that he resonates comes from deep inside, from a life that is fulfilled. He is a lover of nature and is humbled by its perfection.

Needless to say, the percentage of people who truly create for themselves the absolute fulfillment of their dreams is small. I've heard Orv refer to his life and property as heaven on earth, and that if heaven is anywhere near this good, he will be just fine.

I told him about this book and asked if he would provide me with concepts that he lives by and ideas for others to live happier lives. So, in closing I would like to leave you with his words. Of all the words in this book, I consider these to be extremely important because they come from someone in our own family that in my opinion has accomplished what few on this planet ever have.

- In the process of building your riches, let money be far down the line.
- You can be rich if your wants are few.
- It's a bad feeling to get up in the morning with nothing to do.
- Love your job or find another.
- The best things in life aren't things.
- All seem to search and seek but never find the greatest of gifts, *peace of mind*.

FINALE

"We are what we repeated do."

—Aristotle, 384-322 B.C.

There is a song by the country-western group Diamond Rio. Some of the words are: "We all fall down. It's the getting back up that really counts. We live and we learn to help someone up when it's their turn. Life has only one guarantee, our feet won't always be on the ground." Life has its ups and downs. If we're knocked down from time to time, we need to simply keep getting back up. Everything is a stage that shall pass to make way for the next. Richard Carlson says:

"...That everything—the good and bad, pleasure and pain, achievements and mistakes, fame and shame—all come and go. Everything has a beginning and an ending.... Every experience you have ever had is over. Every thought you've ever had, started and finished. Every emotion and mood you've experienced has been replaced by another.... It's enormously helpful to experiment with the awareness that life is just one thing after another. One present moment followed by another present moment. When something is happening that we enjoy, know that while it's wonderful to experience the happiness it brings, it will eventually be replaced by something else, a different type of moment. If that's okay with you, you'll feel peace even when the moment changes. And if you're experiencing some type of pain or displeasure, know that this too shall pass."

The only real constant is change. If our goal is to grow and to deepen our character, we will be able to stay on top of the ebb and flow of life. Be light-hearted, be concerned for others, help them when you can, and don't take yourself too seriously. Joy and true happiness comes from inside. It is not dependent on whether the sun is out, what the stock market does, or any outer condition.

Keep things light by remembering the poster that says, "Life is a test. It is only a test. Had this been a real life you would have been instructed where to go and what to do."

There is a newspaper comic that has a picture of a very distraught-looking lady coming into her therapist's office. The caption reads, "I'd be just fine if good things would start happening to me."

Then there is Woody Allen's quote, "If only God would give me some clear sign! Like making a deposit in my name in a Swiss bank account!"

Once again, the point that is being humorously made is that happiness comes from within. We must not depend on good things happening to us to be happy. If we are happy with who we are, all outer conditions are secondary.

This work obviously is by no means a complete guide to living. In the scope of things, it is but a scratch. It has been said there is a book in each of us. Well, this is my humble attempt, an inventory of my beliefs after having lived half of a century. My goal has been to simply provide some guidance and to share personal perspectives with the hope they will assist you in living a happy, high-quality, fulfilled life.

Take whatever applies and whatever you can use from this work and leave the rest. My goal was to publish this book. Surely it is a long way from perfect, but if a concept rings true, great. If not, so be it. My hope is that maybe you would read it every few years.

Know that it was a work of love and is my gift to you. Know that you are loved, you are worthy, and you can create whatever kind and quality of life you want.

Always be learning and growing and loving until the day you die, and your spirit will never grow old.

All My Love,

Dad

RECOMMENDED READING

"Nature and books belong to the eyes that see them."

—Ralph Waldo Emerson, 1803-1882

Rich Dad Poor Dad by Robert Kiyosaki
The Future of Love by Daphne Rose Kingma
The One-Minute Millionaire by Mark Victor
     Hanson and Robert Allen
Awaken the Giant Within by Anthony Robbins
Choice Theory by Dr. William Glasser
The Game of Life and How to Play It by Florence
     Schinn
The I of the Storm by Gary Simmons (This book
     "saved" me during my life's toughest time.)

Think and Grow Rich by Napoleon Hill (Highest-selling book of all time, second only to the Bible.)

The Turning of the Tide (video or two-cassette album) by David Icke

How I Found Freedom in an Unfree World by Harry Browne

The Instant Millionaire by Mark Fisher

How to Think Like a Millionaire by Mark Fisher and Marc Allen

There Are No Incurable Diseases by Dr. Richard Schulze

Early to Rise e-newsletter, www.earlytorise.com

The O'Reilly Factor by Bill O'Reilly

Dr. Mercola e-newsletter, www.mercola.com

The Road Less Traveled by M. Scott Peck, M.D.

The Trick to Money Is Having Some by Stuart Wilde

Pathways to Peace slide presentation, www.pathways-to-peace.com

Compass of the Soul by Lynn A. Robinson

Printed in the United States
22709LVS00001B/355-363